Brown S.W S

24 JUN 1985

8 NOV 1985

6 FEB 1986

7 MAR 1986

4 JUN 1986 P

6 MAR 1987 P

11 JUN 1987 P

N. McGREGOR

E Wray

AS LUCK WOULD HAVE IT

A Memoir of Sir Leslie Fry

AS LUCK WOULD HAVE IT

A Memoir

by

SIR LESLIE FRY

K.C.M.G., O.B.E.

PHILLIMORE

Published by

PHILLIMORE & CO., LTD.

London and Chichester

Head Office: Shopwyke Hall,
Chichester, Sussex, England

ISBN 0 85033 314 8

Printed in Great Britain by
UNWIN BROTHERS LTD.
at The Gresham Press, Old Woking, Surrey

and bound at
NEWDIGATE PRESS LTD.
at Book House, Dorking, Surrey

CONTENTS

Research and additional text by
Joyce Wilson

LIST OF ILLUSTRATIONS

INTRODUCTION

To write the foreword to the memoirs of a man who had four professions in his lifetime, and whom I was to meet only as he approached the peak of his fourth and last career as diplomat, has been to me a daunting task. I have resolved it by the decision to concentrate not on the earlier years, with which the book itself deals in some detail, not on the themes of the later years, which Leslie's own colleagues have described with great insight in its second half, but on the varied features of his personality and character.

My husband was working on his memoirs until he died, and the ironic, humorous choice for the title—*As Luck Would Have It*—was his own. On the very day of his death he was also actively involved in the subject closest to his heart, in the B.B.C. radio coverage of the Hungarian Revolution of 1956. It was in fact when he was Head of the Eastern Section of the Foreign Office in London, one year before his posting to Budapest, that we were married, and on our arrival there I found myself as Head of Mission's wife with a Revolution at my door. The importance to my husband of the Hungarian people, and the outcome of those days, together with his determination to finish his memoirs in the face of increasing ill health, are the two factors that have convinced me that I should see the book through to completion. It is undoubtedly what he would have wished.

In assembling the book for publication I have been greatly helped by two colleagues who shared those years in Hungary—Lt.-Colonel Noel Cowley and Group Captain Dennis David. For material on Brazil I have to thank Bobbie Evans; in addition thanks are due to my husband's own researcher, Joyce Wilson, B.A., now a historical novelist, who worked closely with him for the last two months of his life on the whole project. Without her application to the task of the remaining research the book would indeed not have been written, and I have much for which to thank her, and the above contributors.

I am especially glad that we were able to complete the memoirs in the way my husband would have wished when I read in the late Selwyn Lloyd's recently published *Suez 1956* that one of the reasons why *he* wrote his memoirs was that his 'account had been missing from the record'. Such was also the case when my husband commenced his own research, only to find that his papers 'had been lost': papers that told the truth about the Hungarian Revolution, and on which was based Leslie's final report to the United Nations, so valued a document that it became known internationally as 'Le Rapport Fry'.

It was in fact Selwyn Lloyd himself, the then Foreign Minister, who called my husband for consultations soon after the Revolution, and informed him that it had been on his own recommendation that Leslie had been posted to Budapest as Minister Plenipotentiary. It is ironical that there is not one word on Hungary in Selwyn Lloyd's *Suez 1956*, when it is now generally acknowledged that Suez took the eyes of the world away from the plight of the Hungarian people at the hands of Russia.

This type of difficult assignment, and there were many such in a remarkable career, brought out Leslie Fry's outstanding qualities. He was perhaps first a soldier and secondly a diplomat, and his early military training and experience stood him in good stead throughout his life. High principles, kindness and loyalty, made him a good friend—and he had many friends. And his quite extraordinary career left the humility, which was also a facet of his nature, quite unchanged. A senior member of Embassy staff under Leslie wrote on one occasion: 'Sir Leslie looks after the staff . . . he appreciates the value of others, and his staff loyally serve him and willingly so, and those who serve him are the better for it'. I would also like to quote Lord Selkirk's charming letter to me on Leslie's demise: 'Leslie's frank and effective way of doing business has been of very real value to this country; if anyone could have made an impression on Sukarno it was he—as no doubt he did in those most difficult times. The keenness of his mind, and the vision with which he entered into all that he did, remains a vivid memory to me'.

Not the least of the qualities which received tribute from Leslie's colleagues was his ability to write, and there is no doubt that had he lived he would have completed an important book as a contribution to the literature on modern Hungary. Whenever he wrote, or spoke, it was with great clarity and quiet authority, and he was always deeply concerned with the problem of promoting understanding—between people of different race or colour or viewpoint. His gift for expression was surely a legacy from his formative years at the Royal Masonic School for Boys at Bushey (now closed), and he was grateful to that organisation all his life, considering it to have been a sheet anchor to all those who had attended the school.

When Leslie was awarded the K.C.M.G., he received amongst many letters of congratulation a letter that particularly pleased him, from Sir Allan Noble, the then Ambassador to Mexico. 'There are various kinds of K.C.M.G', Sir Allan wrote. 'Some go with particular appointments; others are not much more than long service decorations; a remaining few are for really outstanding work: it is so much easier to congratulate the recipient of one in the last class. Your work in Budapest over the Revolution must have earned you yours many times over and I am so glad to be able to send you my warmest and most sincere congratulations.'

To end on a personal note, I am glad to be able in this introduction to record some mention of my many happy memories in both private and public life with my husband. Our good marriage, with great affection on both sides, was reinforced by great diversity of shared experience and, with humility, knowing that I gave him more happiness than anyone or anything else, I can reflect on our wonderful relationship permanently now, in the pages of this book.

Gorehill House, 1978   PENELOPE, LADY FRY

Chapter One

1908-1928

In the late summer of the year 1876 a young schoolteacher of dark good looks, determined spirit, and Victorian principle, buried her husband, Alfred Fry, in the new cemetery at Cork in Ireland. According to one of the solemn customs by which the Victorian observed the whole pageant of death, she herself composed an 'In Memoriam' which has survived in the elegant, fading script of a journal treasured in later years by her grandson.

> There lies a lonely grave, far far away
> Where he I dearly loved lies calmly sleeping,
> And well can I recall the bitter day
> I left him there secure in God's own keeping.

Alfred Fry, grandfather of Leslie Alfred Charles Fry, the subject of this memoir, had died prematurely—and literally in the saddle—on an excursion to Cork from Dublin in his capacity as Lieutenant and Riding Master to the Royal Irish Constabulary. Before joining the Constabulary he had served from 1858, at the age of 18, to 1875, in the splendid Fifth Dragoon Guards. His whole life, as we see it from the formal poses of the sepia photographs and the militaria and insignia that he left, was in the stalwart, military tradition that at least two of his sons—and certainly his grandson, Leslie—were to follow.

Kate Georgina (née Stewart) Fry, Alfred's widow, was herself an 'army schoolmistress'. It was typical of her, and of many of the Fry women since—that once 'on the strength' as the wife of a soldier she proved herself rather more than a cypher. The Fry women do not seem to have been content with the social image of decorative or self-effacing womanhood. And their men seem more often than not (as we see from their portraits) to have chosen them at first for their undeniably, universally pretty faces but, at the same time, to have sensed the character that lurked beneath!

Married at 17, Kate Georgina had already lost two infants, both in their first year. But this was quite usual in a time of high infant mortality figures. She was now alone with three small boys: Maxwell, the youngest; Charles, aged three at his father's death; and the eldest, Alfred, aged five. Four years later, still not yet 30 years old, she received an official army posting like any other member of the service. At the

1

time she was running the Battalion School for the 1st Battalion Rifle Brigade at Aldershot. Now she was to move, with the Battalion, to India.

The diary of the journey out to the sub-continent has survived in her own handwriting, a touching essay in courage. Reading between the lines one can guess at the ordeal, the possible doubt. But this is only between the lines. Many years later her grandson, Leslie Fry, wrote of the Victorians' moral conviction of rightness, whether as parents, teachers, or colonisers. Kate Georgina was, temporarily, all three. And, as Leslie Fry surmised, the sense of rightness was a great source of strength.

When Leslie Fry planned the autobiography which he was unable, through illness, to complete, he stated that the book would not aspire to be History with a capital 'H'. When he talked of a personal and where possible light-hearted account of his own career he had not pursued the idea to its conclusion: it so happened that 'as luck would have it' that career took him at every turn to a spot in the globe or a situation behind the scenes where it was precisely History with a capital 'H' that was going on. And yet in the personal chronicle left by Kate Georgina there is perhaps exactly the note Leslie himself would have struck in the telling, and the episode itself is as pertinent an historical document as the most determined researcher could hope to unearth.

The night before she sailed from Portsmouth Kate Georgina sat in her small, neat cabin in the troopship, surveying the four beds made up for herself and the three boys. That afternoon the Colonel of the Regiment and his wife—the then Duke and Duchess of Connaught—had called to shake her by the hand and present her with an album containing their own, signed photographs. Again, the ceremonial was typical of the Victorian sense of occasion, and of the closeness with which an army widow could expect to be guarded and helped by her husband's colleagues. It was certainly an incident that the middle boy, Charles, was to remember all his days. We do not know why in the end the whole family did not travel together as seemed to have been originally planned. The boy Maxwell certainly stayed on in England, much to his mother's distress later when he became ill. But Charles, who was to become a compulsive traveller as an adult, is recorded as thoroughly enjoying the voyage out, and especially the gift of an orange from the groves of Malta, and the privilege of a glass of sherry with the sumptuous Christmas dinner served on board. It was to be two years before they returned to the United Kingdom.

A subsequent posting to the Sandymount Barracks, Dublin, as schoolmistress to the families of the 2nd Battalion Royal West Kent Regiment stationed there brought the family into the circle in which the eldest boy, Alfred, was eventually to meet his wife. In his mother's class that year was a small girl named Louisa Stoakes. She had a sister, Florence Rose. By strange coincidence Louisa was to become the spinster Victorian aunt who many years later took into her care, and was a major influence on, Leslie Alfred Charles Fry.

In the meantime, Alfred, Kate Georgina's eldest boy, joined the 2nd Battalion Scots Guards at the age of 14, and early in the 1890s trans- ferred to the 2nd Battalion South Wales Borderers, with whom he served throughout the South African War. He was 25 years old, with the rank of Colour Sergeant Instructor, when he married Florence Rose Stoakes, 24 years old—an enchantingly pretty schoolteacher—just before Christmas in the year 1905, at the church of Holy Trinity in the parish of Brompton in Kent. On the 17th April 1908, their son Leslie was born. The couple seem to have settled after the wedding in the district of Abergavenny in Wales, where Alfred was stationed. The town is given as his place of residence on their marriage certificate. It was certainly from there that their small son waved goodbye—on the Abergavenny railway station platform—as his father's Territorial Battalion departed for active service in the 1914 European war. The scene provided one of Leslie Fry's earliest memories.

Surviving heavy casualties suffered by the Battalion (so serious were the losses that it, in fact, never re-formed), Leslie's father was mentioned four times in despatches, and went on, as a volunteer member of the Royal Flying Corps, to play an adventurous role in the latter stages of the war. One of his last leaves, however, was for the tragic purpose of the funeral of his young wife. Florence died totally unexpectedly, of com- plications during an operation for peritonitis. It was May, 1918.

Thirteen months later, apparently making a quite satisfactory recovery from the effects of a war that had taken toll of men's health as well as their lives, Leslie's father went home once more on leave, for the purpose of convalescence. But the recovery had, it seemed, been a temporary, artificial rallying. By June 1919 Leslie, then aged 11, and his young sister, Betty (Margaret Betty Kate), aged five, had lost both their parents.

In the account he has left of his childhood and the influences that in part served to shape his character and attitudes, Leslie Fry mentions with affection that 'British Institution without which no Victorian family was complete: the Victorian Spinster Aunt'. It was Aunt Louise, or 'Louie', the small girl who had sat at Kate Georgina's feet, and who was herself now the headmistress of a school in Esher and resident in 'The School House, Esher' no less, who became parent-guardian and mentor to the young Fry children. Her apparently severe image no doubt reflected her attitude to Learning, and no one in the School House ever neglected their homework. If you did not know Latin or Greek you were not for Aunt Louie. Under her guidance Leslie acquired a capacity for hard work, discipline, and disciplined prose. But the outward severity most certainly concealed real concern for the children who were now her family, Nor did Leslie deny in his spinster Victorian institution a quiet sense of humour.

After a few months attending a day preparatory school conveniently close to The School House, Leslie was offered a place at the Royal Masonic School (otherwise the Royal Masonic Institution for Boys) at Bushey, in Hertfordshire. In later life his career abroad, both in the Army and in the Foreign Office, meant that Leslie was not in a position to be actively involved in The Craft in the way in which previous members of the Fry family had been, but all his life he was devoted to the school itself. In fact, during his retirement and even the month before he died he worked with great interest for the school and its pupils.

The history of the Royal Masonic Institution for Boys has from the start been a story of pastoral care. In 1798 it was founded for the purpose of 'Clothing and Educating the sons of indigent Freemasons', and six boys were soon under its wing. In the early 1800s the Grand Lodge of the Duke of Atholl, who had in the meantime become the school's Patron, voted considerable sums to it. In 1809, to commemorate the accession of George III to the throne, the Board voted a sum of £210 to enable the numbers of the school to be increased to fifty. The prefix 'Royal' was assumed in 1832, when William IV became the school's Patron. And at her death in 1901 Queen Victoria herself, Patron since 1852, was the oldest annual subscriber.

Until the mid-19th century, however, there were no plans for a school as such. The Institution continued to care for and aid financially the sons of The Craft in need—and to place them usually in schools conveniently close to their homes. But by 1857 a building fund established five years earlier enabled Lordship House, at Wood Green, Tottenham, on the outskirts of London, to be adapted as a boarding school, and within two years all 70 of the children now in the Institution's care were received into the school. So rapid and steady from then on was the growth of the school that by 1896 it was decided by the Governors, the funds having also increased with time to the required healthy level, that the purchase of a new site of 67 acres at Bushey could go ahead. The foundation stone was laid ceremonially by the Duke of Connaught in May 1900.

It was characteristic of Leslie Fry that when working with his researcher for his autobiography he jokingly suggested that he might change the title from 'As Luck Would Have It' to 'From Orphanage to Embassy', and it is of interest to consider how many men who start life with the loss of parents do in fact display extraordinary ambition and drive. But his more serious assessment of the school's overall purpose shows an approach to education that was hardly that of the Diplomatic Service pre-war. He wrote that the school was of considerable educational interest because, though its staff, buildings, facilities, playing fields and all other appurtenances bore comparison with those of any (public) school in the kingdom it has always been essentially 'comprehensive'. The entrance examination has never been more than a simple test to ensure that a boy was not beyond all hope of learning, and the family antecedents of its pupils differed widely. 'Their only common denominator', he wrote, 'is that all of them are under the protection of The Craft'.

The common denominator the school itself shared with other Victorian educational establishments was undoubtedly that of the Spartan life.

Even in Leslie Fry's time (1920–26) the life was that of the cold bath syndrome, and it was not unknown for a short run bare-foot in the snow to be considered a good thing. 'Character forming' is perhaps the best way to describe the motivation—if not always the outcome!—of the discipline.

Leslie's own career in the school certainly illustrated the 'comprehensive' scene he himself found of such interest. He worked extremely hard, from a habit inculcated under Aunt Louie's system, but was also a good all-round sportsman. He was keen on the school's 'Modern' curriculum, achieving good Latin translation, and good French composition, as well as winning the English prize in his sixth year. His fencing, which he was to enjoy all his active life, was already very good, and he was captain of cricket and hockey. As Head of School he obviously showed considerable maturity, and the Acting Headmaster (H. R. Francombe) in 1926 wrote that it was a boon to him to have had 'an efficient and tactful' Head of School, and one 'possessed of sound common sense'.

The advent of H. R. Francombe heralded an era of change at Bushey, but it was only one of the many periods of innovation or upheaval that were to mark Leslie Fry's career throughout. He also claimed that he became Head of School 'more by luck than management', and was to claim this for his achievements to come—both in the I.P.S. at the close of the traumatic proceedings by which India gained her independence, and as First Minister in Budapest during the Hungarian Revolution of 1956, to name but two examples.

Leslie's more light-hearted reminiscences of the school include the menu for every day of the week, the antics of a master with a raffish air and a swivel eye who lectured the class on rudimentary betting and form, and the verdict that the combined rigours of Bushey and The School House at Esher produced a boy 'almost entirely untainted by any vestige of sophistication'. He forgot to mention, either jokingly or otherwise, that this stage of his life also produced someone who had such fine command of English that his reports as a member of the Foreign Office were considered to be models of their kind.

The matter of the closure of the Royal Masonic School for Boys is perhaps best dealt with here, as Leslie's involvement with, and loyalty to,

the school continued right into his retirement, and his role in the controversy over the closure was an extension of that involvement and
loyalty. This memoir is not to include a chapter as such on Sir Leslie's
retirement (a word of which he was not too fond), but in the matter of
the school his actions perhaps are best recorded in this section. Co-opted
originally on to the Board of Governors, he was active and articulate in
both routine and controversial matters of organisation and policy. He
contributed greatly to the argument on the retention of Latin as an
important part of the 'Modern' curriculum when this came under fire
in the early 1970s. He was unceasing in his concern for the pupils in
general, and in particular, and as late as four weeks before his death,
when he was clearly desperately ill, he was personally engaged in finding
and selecting places and schools for boys who were to be displaced by
the closure of Bushey.

Like all other Old Boys, Sir Leslie was sentimentally in favour of the
retention of the school, but he held the view that if its future was
economically unsound then something must be done—before it was
too late. The dispute and heart-searching that characterised both the
opposing factions in this matter was in Sir Leslie's own case qualified
by considered, down-to-earth analysis of the crippling situation in which
the school found itself. His writings on the subject, and the answers from
his critics, are in the records of the Institution. Those close to him at
this time have also been anxious to record the conflict he experienced
and which he nevertheless characteristically put on one side when it
came to the need for real decision. The fact that he followed up that
decision with practical effort to redeem where it was possible and to
see—well ahead—that the boys who had to be moved to new schools were
still so placed with care and thought was, if we refer again to the terms
of the Institution's foundation, entirely in the tradition of the school
itself, and also happened to be typical of Sir Leslie's ability to see a
thing through.

*   *   *   *   *

Perhaps the first Old Boy from the Institution to get into the Royal
Military Academy at Sandhurst (the lists show Wellington, Eton, Marl-
borough and Harrow have done rather better!) Leslie was in fact following
the family military tradition in his choice of a career. A study of records
of parentage and professions showed at that period that still half of the
cadets had fathers whose career had been in the Army. Leslie—who had
also been a young officer in the School Army Cadets—has recorded an
amusing account of his Army entrance interview, however, which shows
he was not quite yet the young officer cadet-about-town. He remembers
for one thing he wore a brown suit—a thing he would have found unthinkable in London a year or two later. His problems must have been those

of any young man wishing to enter a profession in order to make a good living as well as out of a sense of family tradition, and in the good years that followed he probably forgot that the one brown suit was the uniform —if not the only suit—of most of the pupils at Bushey. But he gives a disarmingly frank account in the same notes of one of his *faux pas* at the interview. Trying to make something of the rather restricted holidays in the School House at Esher (where he usually applied himself to homework under Aunt Louis's encouragement to be top of the class), he mentioned that he 'went riding about the country'.

'Ah', said a large cavalry general hopefully, 'I suppose the local farmers lend you horses?'

'No', replied Leslie, frank unto the last. 'I meant that I bicycled.'

As a general indication of the 18 months that were to follow, Leslie liked to use A. de Vigny's phrase 'Servitude et grandeur militaires'. He entered the Royal Military Academy, Sandhurst, as a King's Cadet (which meant that he was one of the cadets both meriting and needing a full 'scholarship' for the duration of the course), and as a Prize Cadet. Along with the other 499 gentlemen cadets of 'the R.M.C.' he did not seem unduly bothered by the fairly gloomy prospects of advancement in the money-starved Army of the day. Just as he threw himself into school life, he now immersed himself in the new régime. It amused him that there was little of what he now called 'scholastic nonsense' about the course. The 'Halls of Study', which he describes as dingy classrooms, were used exclusively for arms drill on wet days. 'Strategy', a subject allotted no more than the occasional hour in a lecture theatre, he found was based on the first six weeks of the 1914–18 war. This in a college that had trained Montgomery, Churchill, Horrocks—and, of course, David Niven!

Leslie's description of 'Field Engineering' has something of Niven's own philistine humour. It seems to have consisted of marching over a wasteland named after Barossa (a battle in the Peninsular War) in brown dungarees to dig trenches, fill them in again, and march home. Of the more academic side to life at R.M.C. he wrote:

> The only academic item in the curriculum that I can recall was 'the volun-tary subject'. This did not mean that you could take or leave it, but simply that you had a choice between Military History and French. As I liked reading military history anyway, I chose French. Our tutor was a most agreeable Captain of Chasseurs, resplendent when in uniform, and counting the Military Cross (British) among his decorations. Usually, however, he wore civilian clothes and would cut his sessions short by saying he had an urgent appointment in London. He was sorry to leave, but we might care to fill in time, he would explain in his excellent English, by glancing at the improving copies of such journals as *La Vie Parisienne* which he would then hand round. This regime worked to the satisfaction of us all. We could hardly have been given a better literary inducement to learn his language and he had no failure in the examinations, which he himself conducted.

Among the other luminaries of the R.M.C. of those inter-war years was the legendary Coldstreamer Sergt. Major Brittain, later known as 'The Voice', and Leslie has one or two anecdotes of life with this eccentric, formidable man which do not appear in many of the popular accounts of him.

> The Adjutant of the R.M.C. was the elegant Captain F. A. M. (Boy) Browning of the Grenadier Guards, later Lt. General Sir Frederick Browning, who was to command the First British Airborne Corps in Operation Market Garden, the action at Arnhem in September 1944. He was also to marry Miss Daphne du Maurier. In our first week he gave the Juniors, the new entry, a brief talk. One of the things he said was that His Majesty King George V liked his Army Officers to wear moustaches.
>
> When Sergeant Major Brittain had marched No. 4 Company Juniors back to our lines he gave us his own version of this.
>
> 'Now, Gentlemen, you heard what the Adjutant said. The King wants you all to grow moustaches. Well, I can't *order* you to do this; and even if I did, you'd still need the help of God Almighty. But I can, and I do, order you not—repeat *not*—to shave your upper lips!
>
> For weeks thereafter he would peer closely into our faces as he passed down the ranks. 'Mr. Smith, Sir, you're doing well—very encouraging indeed . . .'. And a few paces later, 'Mr. Brown, Sir, you can't be trying. Are you sure you haven't been shaving?' Somehow or other, all of us managed to grow moustaches.
>
> A friend of mine was tall, thin and angular. No matter how hard he tried, no matter how short his hair, no matter how brightly his belt and buttons shone, he never looked neat and tidy. This disturbed Brittain very much. For days he tried adjusting the young man's tunic, cap and belt as soon as we got on parade. Then one morning even he gave up. He merely stood in front of the boy and said sorrowfully 'Mr. Buncombe-Jefferson, you awful-looking gentleman . . .'
>
> My friend was killed in the rear-guard action at Dunkirk.

Notwithstanding such stories as these, it is clear that Leslie believed that the cadets were given a superbly thorough training as private soldiers: their training as officers was left to their future Commanding Officers, Adjutants and Company Commanders; they accepted and grew to be proud of the discipline which brought them to a state of parade-ground perfection certainly up to and probably beyond that even of the Brigade of Guards. They were good, they knew it, and they enjoyed it.

The passing-out parade of Leslie Fry's term at the R.M.C. took its traditional form, observed to this day, ending with the Adjutant riding his grey horse up the front steps of the Old Buildings while the band played 'Auld Lang Syne'. The Cadets went their separate ways for the Christmas holidays and waited impatiently to be commissioned as Second Lieutenants in His Majesty's Land Forces.

Their tailors meanwhile took measurements for uniforms, but naturally could not finish making them until they knew the Corps into which they were being gazetted.

Leslie had applied for the Indian Army, into which he was duly commissioned on the 2nd February 1928. Money was one reason for his choice, because even in a British Regiment of the Line a private income of, say, £200 a year was desirable. Better prospects of active service and even in peace-time quicker promotion were others. Together with 34 other brand-new Second Lieutenants, a number of older officers, and over 1,000 Other Ranks, mainly R.A.F., he sailed from Southampton a month later for India in H.M. Troopship *Dorsetshire*. Three weeks later they landed in Bombay. It was the height of the period which the media have now taught us all to call 'The Raj', and for 20 years Leslie Fry was to become totally involved in the military, political and social scene that was the last 20 years of the British in India.

Chapter Two

INDIA – 1928-1946

The Army and the Indian Political Service

Once in India, 'Bunny' Fry spent his first year on the customary 'unattached list' before joining a permanent regiment or corps, and was happy to find himself with the 2nd Battalion The Cameronians (Scottish Rifles). This was the old '90th', raised in 1794 by Thomas Graham, later General Lord Lynedoch. The latter's name has also gone down in military history as the founder of the United Service Club in the memorable year of 1815. The use of the appellation 'Scottish Rifles' for the Battalion was intended to distinguish it from the first Battalion, the 26th.

The Cameronians, at the time of 'Bunny' Fry's arrival in India, were stationed in Razmak. This was the barren hill country of Waziristan on the North West Frontier, and the settlement was surrounded by walls of boulders within which stood pillars of electric lights, very much like a security boundary in a prison camp! The garrison consisted of one battalion of British Infantry, and five battalions of the Indian Army. There was also the usual range of ancillary units, including several batteries of Mountain Artillery, their guns carried in picturesque fashion on pack-mules—the only way in which they could hope to stay mobile in this stony, ridge landscape.

There seems to have been very few of the amenities of civilisation at this posting, and even Sandhurst must have appeared at a distance as a haven of luxury. The barracks, and officers' quarters, of the Upper Camp were constructed of bricks, mortar, and corrugated iron. Officers and men inhabiting the even less luxurious Lower Camp had to be content with tents walled in dried mud—essential addition for insulation against the snowfalls and bitter cold of the Frontier winters. There was, however, a small bazaar where life's little necessities could be bought, in the Upper Camp.

Yet in this far-flung outpost of British civilisation, where even the main parade ground was nicknamed the Aerodrome in token of its barren expanse, the Battalion did not go without that symbol of leisure and sportsmanship: the golf course. Leslie Fry had entertaining memories of playing on this hazardous 'green', which straggled up the hillside adjacent to the parade ground, hardly concealing its rock-strewn surface with a veneer of sifted ashes. Equipped with special leather tees for every shot except those taken on 'the ashes' (*alias* the green), the players remained unsurprised if a ball ricocheted off a rock and came to rest behind instead of fore—or if a straying Pathan tribesman took a quite different shot at the players from the hills. Being a Scottish regiment, of course, the players took their game—even in such a setting—in deadly earnest. There is no record of what was said when Leslie Fry found himself on a runaway horse, crossing the 'green' between his Commanding Officer and the pin!

Another eccentric feature of life at Razmak was the total absence of women of any nationality, and of course the rumours that brave females had made their way disguised—in true camp-follower style—as men, even riding despatch motorcycles to and from their shadowy adventures, were rife. Bunny never actually saw one of these legendary creatures, but he did know that the European women could get as far as Bannu, a cantonment about 70 miles along the heavily-patrolled Frontier road.

The year seemed to go very fast for the young subalterns newly arrived at the Frontier, and there is no doubt that Leslie became attached to the life, and the Battalion. When the time came for him to move on, and join a regiment permanently, he was invited to join the Cameronians by the Company Commander. But by then Leslie was hoping to be allotted one of the (very scarce) vacancies in the 1st Battalion the 4th Prince of Wales' Own Gurkha Rifles.

The 4th, and their linked regiment the 1st King George's Own Gurkha Rifles, were stationed in Razmak at the time, and Leslie had already found particular friends in the Battalion. It is one of the best-known regiments of the former Indian Army, and is of course familiar to the layman through the works of John Masters, especially 'Bugles and a Tiger', which described Masters' own early life with the Regiment. Leslie's own term of service with them was, as it happens, to be shorter than he himself anticipated at first. But it was a link he was never entirely to sever, and in fact, having maintained close contact as a member of the Officers' Association, he took a special interest in the founding of The Gurkha Museum at Queen Elizabeth Barracks, Church Crookham, near Aldershot, in 1974, and in the last month of his life presented ceremonially to the Museum the dress kit which he wore as a young officer.

The purpose of the Gurkha Museum is to commemorate the services of Gurkhas to the British Crown—services which date back to 1814—and it is not surprising that 'Bunny' Fry took to the regimental tradition with such enthusiasm. In his own notes for this memoir, he wrote:.

'Bakloh, in the foothills of the Himalayas above the small Punjab railhead station of Pathankot, was the Regiment's home. Though it was rare indeed for both Battalions to be in Bakloh at the same time, each had their own Lines and, like the rest of the Brigade of Gurkhas, trained their own recruits. During the recruiting season youngsters in groups of eight or ten, to a total of about one hundred for each Battalion, would be brought to the Depot from Western Nepal, the Regiment's recruiting area, by senior non-commissioned officers who had been on leave. Naturally knowing no language other than Gurkhali, which only their own British officers spoke, never having worn boots before, their coats of homespun cloth fastened not with buttons but with tape, each with the indispensable kukri tucked into his waistband, these boys had three qualities in common: courage, good humour and so intense a devotion to soldiering that they could be trained to take their place in the Regiment, no matter where it was serving, in a matter of months. They also had certain frailities not unknown in the British Army: a liking for women, liquor and gambling. Gambling has never attracted me.

In 1931 the Training Company of the 2nd/4th was commanded by Joe Lentaigne, later to succeed Wingate in command of the Chindits and to become a Lieutenant General. At first to my disappointment, I had been given command of the Training Company of the 1st/4th when the Battalion was ordered to Peshawar, but I quickly grew to love the job. There seems to be a strain of the schoolmaster in me.

Jack Masters, who joined the Regiment after I had left it and took on my personal Gurkha servant, Biniram Thapa, has not entirely cornered the market of stories about Gurkhas in general, and the Fourth in particular.

On Christmas morning the pensioners living near Bakloh came to the Mess lawn. The Band played, the rum flowed. The oldest pensioner was a 1st/4th Subadar (a senior Viceroy-commissioned officer) who had been with the Regiment in the famous march from Kabul to Kandahar in 1880, under Major General Sir Frederick Roberts, later Field Marshall Earl Roberts. Now over 80 years of age, the Subadar's hearing and sight were not what they had been but otherwise he was in excellent health and spirits. I invited him to walk round the Mess with me, to see again the Regiment's trophies.

In the Card Room I asked him who that officer was, there in the picture on the far wall.

The old man went across and peered for a moment at the Victorian lithograph, his face wrinkling like a walnut in his concentration. Then he squared his shoulders, took a pace back and saluted smartly. "Bobs Sahib Bahadur", he whispered.

Our efficient and friendly Medical Officer, Clayton, a Captain in the Indian Medical Service, told me that he had admitted into hospital a Gurkha who had turned up from Nepal in an advanced stage of tuberculosis. I went to see the man. He had served with the 1st/4th in France, he explained, and on demobilisation in 1919 had gone back to his remote village in Nepal. Later he had heard that medals were being given to men who had served in the war, but he had never had his. Perhaps he should have come to Bakloh for them before. He had put the journey off. It took many days to walk from his village, over the hills. Now that he was sick he had a second reason for making the journey: he would get good care from the Regiment.

The Senior Gurkha Officer and I checked his name and number in the rolls, together with such other details of his service as we could piece together. If there were any doubt about his claim, and we could see little, he deserved the benefit of it. Yet to extract his medals from Army Head-quarters, using the right form in quintuplicate, would take heaven knew how long; and his time was short.

Subadar Shiam Sing Thapa and I thought of borrowing some medals from a serving officer, but they would have the owner's name on the rims and our man was probably just literate enough to spot it. Subadars, however, are men of infinite resource and long memory. Shiam Sing recalled that a pair of unclaimed 1914–18 War medals, the General Service and the Victory, had for years been lying at the bottom of the Guard Room strong-box. True, they also had names round the rims; but perhaps I could see no objection to his asking the Regimental Armourer to remove them?

Two Gurkha Officers and I, in full Review Order, went down to the Hospital and presented the medals with all ceremony to the man. Some days later, propped up in a leather case on his bedside table, they were the last things he saw.'

                              *   *   *   *   *

However deep the involvement illustrated in these stories had become for Leslie Fry, he did fall victim after the first years in Bakloh to a growing apprehension that if he did not take destiny into his own hands in some manner life was going to take on a pattern of regular, two-yearly oscillations between Bakloh and the hostile Frontier. He had found Bakloh hardly more in contact with the outside world than Razmak, and though it was not customary for a young Indian Army officer to rush into matrimony (mainly for financial reasons) it had been pointed out to him by at least one attractive member of the Bakloh Eouropean community that he could not hope to combine his enjoyment of scrambling up and down barren hills for King and Countty with an acceptable social round. Impecunious subaltern or not, Leslie got the point: and studied with more than casual interest a document circulated by Army Head-quarters about the Foreign and Political Department of the Government of India. Two of his friends who had stayed with the Regiment had volunteered the opinion that had they had their time again (they were some 10 years older than Leslie) they would have switched careers and chosen the 'I.P.S.', or more accurately the Foreign and Political Department of that Service: the 'F and P'.

That was in fact the choice that Leslie now made. In 1933, with considerable heart-searching, he made the decision to give up his career as a professional soldier and join the small service that had been founded in 1783. Recruitment was mainly by nomination, and not always from the Indian Army and the Indian Civil Service. As it happens, Leslie survived not only the interview with Lord Willingdon, the then Viceroy of India, at Viceroy House, New Delhi, but also the scrutiny of Lady Willingdon, and was appointed—on probation—on the 20th November 1933. He had unknowingly taken a step that would lead him, indirectly, to a career as a diplomat, some years later. But in the meantime he entered on a phase of his career that clearly he found absorbing and of some challenge.

The Foreign side of the 'F and P' administered the North West Frontier Province, Baluchistan and the Tribal Areas, staffed the Diplomatic Missions in Afghanistan and Nepal as well as the Consular posts in East Persia and the Persian Gulf, and ran an assortment of Residencies, Agencies and Trade Missions as widely separated as Aden, Kashgar, Tibet, Sikkim and Bhutan. The political side was responsible for conducting relations with the Indian States, the territories of which covered one-third of the sub-continent. Officers could be moved from side to side of the Service, which thus offered a greater variety of work than any other under the Crown.

On the internal side, after six months as personal assistant (a glorified aide-de-camp) to the Hon'ble the Agent to the Governor General in Rajputana, Leslie Fry was posted to Lucknow as Assistant Commission in name, but in fact to be trained in Criminal, Civil and Revenue Law. This was the normal, invaluable start to a young soldier's career in his new Service. Later he served in Hyderabad State (Deccan), in the Punjab States, in the Chhattisgarh States (Central India), and twice in Jammu and Kashmir State.

On the external side, the posts held by Leslie Fry were those of Vice-Consul in Seistan, S. E. Iran, 1946–38; British Joint Commissioner, Ladakh, 1940; Under Secretary to the Government of India in the External Affairs Department, 1941–44; and Deputy Secretary in that Department from 1946 until the transfer of power in 1947. Pandit Jawaharlal Nehru, an aristocratic intellectual with something of the policeman also in his character, was his Minister.

This quite formidable record of appointments that seemed to take Leslie Fry to the right place at the right time, very much an observer—and eventually an active participant—in history in the making, is perhaps fairly typical of career-patterns for the men who served in India in those last 15 years. So much has been written since, and with the 30th anniversary of Independence in 1977, the spur to the media has sharpened, on the theme of The Raj, and had Sir Leslie lived to complete his own memoirs he would most certainly have devoted a section to that curious social-political phenomenon of the British in India as he saw it. As it is, he has left several documents that to some extent illustrate that phenomenon. His story of a tiger hunt stands on its own as a comment, and an adventure, and in the verbatim account that follows perhaps the most valuable element is the sense of fate—an element that tinged more than the tiger hunt and its outcome in the years to come.

*   *   *   *   *

'Conservation is a word which nowadays is on every lip, and usually with justice. Nevertheless, circumstances can alter cases. Even the most dedicated preserver of wild-life would presumably have difficulty in regarding with affection a tiger, for example, which had long plundered the meagre herds and flocks of Indian villages living constantly in the shadow of starvation.

One fine morning in April 1934 a party of young people had walked out from Mt. Abu, the Summer headquarters of the Agent to the Governor General in Rajputana, to Trevor Tal, where they had spent a pleasant day bathing in the lake and picnicking. The roads in and around Mt. Abu were so few and narrow that only Ruling Princes and the A.G.G., my Chief, were permitted motor-cars, and small ones at that. Suddenly round a curve in the road came the Residency car with the wife of the A.G.G. in it.

She told us that a villager had brought in news of a tiger kill. Would I like to go out after the killer? No invitation could have been more welcome.

I went back to the Residency with her, changed into a khaki shirt and shorts, borrowed the A.G.G.'s rifle, along the barrel of which a powerful electric torch was fixed, and set off in the car to that part of the mountain-road closest to the kill. A crowd of villagers had already gathered there.

Unfortunately no professional big-game shikari was in the district and I had therefore asked one of the Residency messengers, a Muslim named Fazal, if he would care to come; he occasionally went to a duck-shoot with me. He accepted at once. No sooner had we set out however than I realised with horror how foolish this invitation had been. I had only my Service .45 revolver with which to arm Fazal, a useless weapon except at short range and in his hand probably not very effective then, for he had no experience of it. What therefore I had thoughtlessly asked him to do was to stake his life on the ability of a novice, using a rifle he had never held before, let alone fired, to shoot the first tiger he had ever encountered. But clearly we could not turn back.

We found that the tiger had killed two buffaloes, about a hundred yards apart, and had eaten the haunch of one. It seemed virtually certain that he had then gone down the hillside to drink at the stream in the valley and to lie quietly in the undergrowth during the heat of the next day. If he returned to the carcasses he thus would probably come first to that which was lower down the slope. We could not be sure of this, however, and nothing would have been more frustrating than to wait for him at one carcass while he made his meal off the other. I accordingly asked the villagers to drag the higher carcass down to within ten or so yards of the other.

That done, they fixed a small wood and plaited-rope bedstead for us into the crotch of a tree from which an unimpeded view of the dead buffaloes could be had. But that was its only virtue, against which had to be set a couple of defects. It was farther than I could have wished from the carcasses; and the sole position we could occupy in it was too low to save us were I either to miss or only to wound the animal; a fully-grown tiger can spring to a height of about thirteen feet from a standing position and will certainly charge while strength is left to it. However, it was a case of Hobson's choice. There was only one tree of any size at all on the edge of the clearing in which the carcasses were lying.

Small boughs were interlaced round the front and sides of the bedstead to form a screen, and Fazal and I then climbed into this rather precarious *machān* to begin our vigil. Having made sure that I could get the rifle easily through an aperture in the screen in front of us, I rested it across my knees.

It was unusual for a tiger to travel so far into the hills from the plains of Rajputana. This one, a large male judging by his pug-marks, was said to have come from Danta a year or so before and had the reputation of being a wanton killer. According to the villagers, he rarely returned to a kill. Having eaten what he would, it seemed that he preferred to leave the rest and seek fresh game.

On past form the chances of his appearing were slender. I was considering how long honour would compel me to sit in cross-legged discomfort, food for a vicious swarm of mosquitoes, when like a pale wraith the tiger materialised noiselessly on the far side of the clearing. It was then about seven o'clock. An almost full moon was rising, though little of its light filtered through the undergrowth. In the dim twilight the illusion of the animal's great size was intensified. He looked enormous, and splendidly beautiful.

He was staring up at the *machān*. Plainly it was something new to him, something he had not expected to see. Fazal and I sat as if turned to stone, waiting to see what would happen and wondering if he would leap up to investigate the strange shape in the tree.

The jungle is never silent for long. Some form of wild-life will move or call. A slight noise came from away to the right of the tiger, perhaps caused by a mongoose scurrying through fallen leaves. The tiger turned his head sharply towards it and as he did so I put the muzzle of the rifle, with the electric torch clamped to it, through the aperture in the screen before us.

Satisfied that the noise represented no danger, the tiger turned his head to the front again and slowly came forward into the clearing without giving us another thought. When he halted over a carcass I took the best preliminary aim I could in the poor light, switched the torch on, the safety-catch off, adjusted my aim and fired.

The animal roared feebly. After the slight wisp of smoke had cleared from the muzzle of the rifle I saw that he was swaying unsteadily and seemed to be mortally wounded. But there was no point in taking a risk; he might be only temporarily disabled, and the recuperative powers of tigers are legendary. I fired again.

The roaring stopped. The animal sank back and rolled out of sight into dense undergrowth.

I reloaded and we waited for about ten minutes, to give the tiger time to show himself again if he were capable of getting to his feet. Then I gave several blasts on a whistle, the pre-arranged signal by which the villagers half-a-mile away would know that I thought it safe for them to approach us.

When they were about fifty yards behind us I shouted to them to halt. It would be sensible to gain more evidence that the tiger was in fact dead before we went forward. I therefore asked Fazal to climb down from the *machān* while I kept my rifle trained on the place at which the tiger had disappeared. Then I transferred the rifle to Fazal, who kept the place covered while I descended. Taking the rifle over again I made my way cautiously towards the area in which the tiger lay hidden from sight.

There he was, stretched out as if asleep. The villagers came up to me with their pressure-lamps and threw stones at him while I kept him covered. No sign of life was left. My bullets had hit him in the neck and chest. He was found later to measure 9 feet 4 inches.

After distributing largesse to all and sundry, with the promise of more when the tiger was brought in, I took Fazal back with me to the Residency, gave him a substantial tip and went off to bath and dress for dinner. Over a drink before the meal my Chief asked me what had happened. I replied that the tiger had appeared but that unfortunately I had missed him . . . The A.G.G. looked at me and said "You're a very unconvincing fibber. I can see from your eyes that you got him. Now, let's have the story."

Fazal's verdict came close to the heart of the matter. On the way home I apologised for thoughtlessly taking him out with nothing better than a revolver in his hand, and said I hoped this had not worried him. No, he assured me, it had not. Kismet—fate—ruled everything, and the Sahib was known to be lucky.'

India—1940 onwards

Notes

1st June 1940
(On hearing the news of Dunkirk)

'It is of course rash to attempt to prophesy, but it seems to me that this very serious reverse may prove to be a blessing in disguise. In Flanders the B.E.F. and the French were fighting to protect the Channel Ports, the advantages of occupying which, without command of the sea, seem doubtful, for the few extra miles so gained by the German Air Force can mean little in these days of long distance flights. With our Armies withdrawn unbeaten in the field and re-formed, we have at our disposal a striking-force for use where we will when the moment for our counter-attack comes. There is certainly no need for pessimism, and my conviction in our ultimate success is unshaken.'

19th June 1940

'On the 18th June we heard the amazing news that the French Government had asked for peace-terms, and that the British Government had offered France a pact of union. To an Englishman the better course is obvious enough, but whether the French view the position in quite the same light is doubtful. Their losses in men and material must have been enormous and their retreat, so far from having been in good order, as the wireless and newspapers assure us, must latterly have been no better than a rout. "Sauve qui peut" and "la trahison" have, I suspect, been the phrases most commonly heard in France in the last few days. It is at present impossible to conjecture why the French poured money like water into the Maginot Line without extending it to the sea, or why they permitted, apparently without counter-attacking, the salient made at Sedan to be widened into an unbridgeable gulf through which the endless stream of German fighting-vehicles has passed into the heart of France.'

22nd June 1940

'Hitler has apparently demanded that French plenipotentiaries be appointed to hear and answer his terms. I imagine the terms will be light in order that the French may have no difficulty in accepting them;

once France is disarmed and unable to resist, Hitler can impose what terms he will, irrespective of any pledge he may for his part have given France. The fate of the French Fleet and, to a lesser extent, that of the Air Force will be a large factor in the future course of the War; but I cannot imagine any Captain of a French vessel, able to steam out to sea and join the British naval forces, tamely surrendering his ship whatever his Government may say.'

26th June 1940

'The French seem to have accepted the German terms, though our wireless set faded out before we could learn what those terms are. We now face the Master of Europe alone—no new position in our history—and so victory when it comes will bring all the greater glory, but God knows at what price. Recriminations would be futile at such a time, but one cannot help marvelling at the apathy of the French and British peoples (I suspect we are the more to blame) that allowed our politicians in the last decade or so to let us decline into this sorry mess.'

Shortly afterwards, this particular series of pronouncements by that little-known authority on military affairs, Captain L. A. C. Fry, was silenced for a time.

'The battery of the wireless set has now failed completely and we have to rely on week-old papers for our news. The War seems very far away.'

Elsewhere he remarks:

'I am reading Pepys' Diary again. It is comforting to see how often he expected defeat, ruin and massacre in our wars only to have his expectations unfulfilled.'

There is enough material in the diary, supported by a selection of facts and figures from sources such as the Central Asian Society, to provide a book on Ladakh. I wonder, however, if many would read it.

*   *   *   *   *

'Orders transferring me from the Kashmir residency had reached me in Leh. I was to go to the Chhattisgarh States Agency as Assistant Political Agent. No sooner therefore had I got back to Srinagar on the 27th August than preparations had to begin for the move.

I arrived in Raipur in the Central Provinces, the headquarters of the Agency, at 5 a.m. on the 1st October 1940. The only accommodation available was a bungalow with no more than one bedroom in it, but this hardly mattered because throughout the year we slept under mosquito-nets on the veranda or, if the weather were dry, in the garden. Eight months of the year were hot, two very hot (115deg. in the shade was no unusual temperature) and two, in the monsoon, very wet.

The Agency consisted of sixteen States, of which Bastar, covered with dense jungle and inhabited mainly by aborigines, was the largest. The Political Agent was one of the most efficient and likeable men in the Service, as well as being a brilliant games-player, and the work I found extremely interesting. Seven of the States were under minority administration, the Agency acting in effect as Regent, four others were under financial control and two more on the verge of it, and the rest required far more help than larger, more nearly self-sufficient States would have needed or been disposed to accept.

A good deal could be written about the dirty, blisteringly hot, fly-infested town of Raipur, regrettably characteristic of many other such places in the plains of India.

Clearly, however, in the sort of book I have in mind one would have to confine oneself to general topics: the changing political circumstances in India, the way of life of the British in India between the Wars, why most of us were there anyhow (an interesting, relatively well-paid and pensionable career about sums it up), and why we left. This section might be called, if the title has not been used already, The Twilight of the Raj.

At all events, I was not long in the Chhattisgarh States Agency. Most unexpectedly in April 1941 I was offered, and of course accepted, the post Under Secretary to the Government of India in the External Affairs Department.

New Delhi, the city built by the British which succeeded Calcutta in 1911 as the capital of India, has a winter climate as agreeable as any in the world, but in summer is decidedly hot. Prickly heat at that season was almost universal among Europeans, for air-conditioning was unknown in India and efficient ceiling fans were none too plentiful. To concentrate by day on one's work, clad in damp clothing, however thin, and at night to try to sleep with a mosquito-net over one's bed in the garden or on the flat roof of one's bungalow, required either considerable determination of purpose or a high degree of insensitivity.

The Government of India were therefore in the sensible if perhaps extravagant habit of removing themselves more of less *en bloc* to Simla for the hot weather. In sublime contrast to the fierce heat of Delhi it ranked among the main pleasures of life to find oneself, after a night's journey by train and a short drive by motor-car up the hillside, in the dank coolness of Simla and to smell lush vegetation instead of dust, to be dry instead of sweating. It is arguable indeed that the expense of the annual move to the hills and back was justified by a larger volume of better work produced by healthier, more contented officials and the staff of Army Headquarters.

Confirmation of my new appointment came through in due course, and I reported to the External Affairs Department on the 7th June. It was the last time that the Government of India were to be in Simla for the hot weather.

When, moreover, the time came to return to Delhi in the autumn of 1941, every civil and military organisation in the capital had so increased in numbers that normal accommodation was impossible to obtain. I was provided with one large tent to live in, two small ones for ablutionary purposes and another to serve as a kitchen. With creditable speed, however, several estates of small but serviceable bungalows were put up, and meanwhile it was probably beneficial to live outdoors.

It is a great pity that I did not continue even intermittently with the diary which I had begun when I set out for Ladakh. One of the last entries in it was made at the end of 1941 and reads:

"The year 1941 has been remarkable mainly for its miscalculations. Indeed, this War seems to have been a series of miscalculations. We have miscalculated many things: France and her Maginot Line, Norway, the effect of a Panzer Division blitz, the possibilities of air-borne invasions, the strength of Japan and our precarious hold on Malaya and Singapore. The enemy have certainly made two serious miscalculations: Britain's almost defenceless position after Dunkirk and Russia's strength and ability to stand firm. Not only did Germany miscalculate Russia's strength. The British General Staff assessed Russian resistance in terms of weeks, not even months, but a year has passed and the U.S.S.R., although they have suffered appalling casualties, are fighting back. I wonder what the history-books will make of it all, 50 years hence."

I held the appointment of Under Secretary in the External Affairs Department for three years.

Its title made the job sound more important than it was. At the head of the Department was the Foreign Secretary, in those days of the Raj not a politician but a very senior member of the Political Service. Next came a Joint Secretary, then a Deputy Secretary and finally that general handyman, the Under Secretary. At one time the list of subjects with which I was expected to cope consisted, I recall, of America, China, the North East Frontier of India, the French and Portuguese Possessions in India and the Prisoners of War camps in India so far as the External Affairs Department was concered with international problems arising in regard to them.

In addition I was the Department's representative for passport and foreign nationality matters, and its link with the Government of India's foreign publicity organisation which was being so ably run by Geoffrey Wheeler, also of the Political Service.

If moreover we could be said to have such an official at all, I was also Chef de Protocol. For commercial and passport purposes and generally to help their nationals with their individual problems, a few countries had for years been permitted to maintain Consular establishments in India, though only in ports, not in New Delhi, the capital; but India's constitutional status at that time precluded her from receiving diplomatic Missions. Our knowledge of the conventions and usages of international diplomacy were therefore restricted, a deficiency we had to make good as we went along and as quickly as possible when representatives of the American and Chinese Governments opened offices in Delhi. To preserve the constitutional niceties they were designated Commissioners, but in all but name were Ambassadors, and they and their staffs expected all customary diplomatic privileges, though ceremony and protocol naturally were reduced in wartime to a bare minimum. This was a part of my multifarious duties I could well have done without.

When the 10th U.S. Army Air Force descended on Delhi the Americans in the city outnumbered the British, or so it seemed. Certainly the American impact on India was considerable and their overt anti-colonial attitude was an embarrassment at times, nationally and personally. It came as something of a shock, for example, to be told by an American journalist with obvious conviction that 'When this war is over we shall have to fight you British'.

After three years, a fairly long time to serve without leave in Delhi and the hectic circumstances of the External Affairs Department in wartime, my health began to decline, though I did not think I was ill enough to report sick. I was accordingly transferred to Srinagar as First Assistant to the Resident in Kashmir, in the hope that I should recover in a better climate.

The decline unfortunately continued. Shortly after Japan's surrender I had to take to my bed. Then I was flown to Delhi in a small aeroplane and transferred to an Army Transport aircraft which had been stripped to the bare essentials in order to carry as many passengers as could be crowded into it. Five very uncomfortable days later I was taken by ambulance from a Service airport to the Seaman's Hospital in East London, which had become one of the main hospitals dealing with tropical illnesses when the Tropical Diseases Hospital in Euston was bombed beyond use. I was told that I could have up to twelve months' leave, in a tone which suggested that I should be lucky to live to take it.

Sprue was the complaint that had struck me, a wasting disease of which the symptoms resemble a combination. of anaemia and severe dysentery. It can be fatal, but more often than not responds favourably to a move from the tropics to a cool, humid climate. Raw liver—which I hate—and strawberries used to figure largely in the prescribed diet.

By the grace of God I quickly recovered. From London I was moved to a Nursing Home in Kent and after a couple of months was discharged, though for a long time I positively rattled with pills and had to visit a Harley Street Specialist regularly.

So much better had my condition become that Colonel Sir Denholm Fraser of the Political Service, Political Aide-de-Camp to the Secretary of State for India, asked me early in 1946 if I would be able to act for him while he accompanied the Cripps Mission to India. I gladly accepted.

One of my duties, which in all conscience were light enough, was to look after the Indian Princes and potentates who were about to visit England for the Victory celebrations. It was for this reason that I had the honour of being one of the half-dozen Stewards in the Royal Box at the Victory Parade in London. Shortly afterwards I was also on duty in the Royal Box at Ascot during the first meeting to be held there since the war.

My appearance on the fringe of duty gave an idea to some or other of my friends in Delhi, causing the new Foreign Secretary to send me a telegram. Its gist was that if I now were fit enough, and only on that condition, he would offer me the job of Deputy Secretary in the External Affairs Department when Dem Fraser returned shortly to the India Office and I was on leave again.

Foolish perhaps I have been about neither asking for nor declining appointments, but I was not foolish enough to rush back to India without medical approval. Indeed, I do not think I should have been permitted to do so. Had I, and then fallen victim once more to Sprue, it would have brought down a good deal of criticism on the India Office from the medical authorities and particularly from the Treasury, concerned more with paying for officials than providing for ill ones or, even worse, for widows and orphans.

The Harley Street specialist questioned me at considerable length. Physically I could do with longer at home, he then said, in a cool climate and on an English diet. Mentally however it was clear that I should be unhappy if I did not return to duty. The appointment in Delhi obviously attracted me, and he would take my word for it that we were about to see the end of the Indian Empire; he realised how anxious I was to be in the capital during those historic days. He decided that the mental considerations outweighed the physical, and understanding attitude for which I was grateful.

Shortly afterwards I was on my way back by air to Delhi and the familiar, friendly surroundings of the External Affairs Department.

The other day, looking through some reference books in the excellent public library in Petworth, I noticed a Medical Dictionary and looked up "Sprue" in it. The disease sounded as unpleasant as I remembered it, but the last sentence of the entry carried a warning I had not heard before. "An individual who has had Sprue should never return to residence in the tropics unless it is absolutely essential".

After returning to India in 1946 I was to serve more than another ten years in the tropics. One must follow one's star.'

Chapter Three

GAME DIARY

Kept by Leslie Fry

'On the evening of December 2nd, 1933, I left for Danta State with the A.G.G. by train. We detrained at Abu Road early the next morning, and proceeded by motorcar. The Maharana of Danta (Maharana Shri Bhawani Singhji) met us on the way, and told us that he had arranged a little rough shooting for us. Three small "beats" ensued, which produced a "bag" of two hares and four jungle-fowl, of which I was lucky enough to get one hare and two of the jungle-fowl. There were some six guns, including, of course, Colonel Ogilvie and the Maharana.

I had not shot a jungle-fowl before this. After lunch, the Maharana told Col. Ogilvie that "khabar" of two panther had been brought in by villagers, and asked him if he would care to try for one. Col. Ogilvie, having shot so many panthers, asked to be excused, but kindly said that I would like to go—much to my delight. At 4 p.m. I set off accompanied by Maharaj Lal Singh of Banswara, who was staying with the Maharana, in one of the State cars. We went some 5 miles, and then went on foot into the low hills. The *machān* was built in a large tree, immediately in front of which was a precarious platform, made of rough matting on four poles, on top of which was tied a live kid. The idea of placing the kid on the platform was to prevent hyaenas killing it.

We climbed into the *machān*, and settled down to wait. Night fell, and as no panther had appeared, we returned to the Guest House. Fruitless though our wait was, it had been of great interest to me, since it was my first experience of panther-shooting—or perhaps I should say, of attempting to shoot panther.

The next morning, the 4th December, we left the Guest House immediately after breakfast, and visited the dwelling of a Sādhu, who has sat there, completely naked, and covered with ashes, for 12 years. He never speaks, and takes two pounds of goat's milk a day to keep himself alive. We sat, shoeless, in front of him for a few minutes in complete silence, and then left to shoot.

The morning's bag totalled 6 hares, 12 jungle-fowl, and 2 partridge, of which I managed to obtain 3 hares, and 3 fowl. Danta is covered with thick jungle, and is really extremely beautiful in its way. I enjoyed the morning very much indeed.

After lunch, the Maharana kindly suggested that I should try at the other place from which news of panther had come. Accordingly, I left with his Shikari, at about 3.30 p.m. We arrived at the *machān* at 4.15, and climbed into it. It was exactly like the former one, yesterday.

At 5.15, I saw, away up on the hill-side, the head and shoulders of the beast as it stood motionless peering out of the undergrowth—my first sight of a live panther, other than in a Zoo. It stood there, surveying the scene, for quite 10 minutes, and then stepped slowly clear of the bushes. It lay down in the sun beneath a large rock about 150 yards from us, and I could have tried to shoot it then, but I felt that it would certainly approach nearer, and afford me an easier shot. I had no wish to return to Camp with the humiliating news that I had missed my first panther!

With my eyes glued to the panther, and contracting acute cramp rapidly, I squatted motionless. The Shikari, quite blasé, wanted me to shoot then, but I preferred to wait.

At 6 p.m., when I was in despair, since the light was failing, the panther leisurely arose, and very slowly moved down the hill. It disappeared into the bushes again, and I sat in an agony of apprehension lest it should be alarmed, and leave entirely. However, my fears were set at rest, for it reappeared some 60 yards away from us, directly in front of the *machān*. It very, very slowly moved towards the goat, which seemed entirely oblivious of any danger. When the panther was about 50 yards away, moving slowly and carrying its head low, I fired. I was really very surprised, and very thrilled, to see it topple over and lie still. I fired again, at the Shikari's suggestion—"to make assurance doubly sure". The time then was 6.15 p.m. and had I waited longer, the light would have failed. As it was, I could barely see the foresight.

We climbed down from the *machān*, and cautiously approached the panther, rifles in hand. My first shot had struck the beast in the forehead, killing it instantly. It proved to be a female. The goat was taken off by its owners, and will never, I understand, be required to undergo such a hazardous ordeal again, now that it has passed unscathed through one. The villagers put the dead panther in the back of the car, and I returned to the Guest House—not a little jubilant, be it confessed!

The panther measured 6 feet 2 inches, which is, the Maharana told me, an average size for a female panther in Danta. He has arranged for the skin and skull to be sent to Van Ingen for me.

The following morning we again had a short shoot, but got only 1 hare, 1 partridge, and one jungle-fowl—to which bag I contributed the partridge.

We left Danta for Erinpura after the shoot, visiting the shrine of Ambaji, and the Jain Temples at Gomaria. The latter contain some very wonderful and delicate old carvings.

On the 8th December I accompanied Col. and Mrs. Ogilvie to Bharatpur, for the bi-annual Duck Shoot. We stayed with Mr. and Mrs. L. G. L.

Evans, at the Agency; Mr. Evans' brother; Mr. Wingate, the Joint Secretary of the Foreign and Political Department; Mr. and Mrs. Wylie (Prime Minister in Alwar); and Captain and Mrs. Carroll, were also guests in the house.

At 9.30 a.m. on the 9th we set off for the jheels, which are the most extensive I have ever seen. At 10 a.m. the bugle sounded the "Commence Fire", The birds flew very high, and there were not nearly so many as there have been at previous shoots. We shot until 12 o'clock, and then from 3 p.m. onwards. I left with the A.G.G. at 4.30, and returned to tea. There were 50 guns, and the bag, which has once exceeded 4000 birds, totalled 551. I, I regret to say, could only muster 5 birds as my share— 2 Common Teal, 1 Shoveller, 1 Nukhta, and 1 Pochard. I found it incredibly difficult to hit them, and wasted an enormous number of cartridges on birds which were too high. Evans obtained 30 birds, which was, I think the highest individual bag. The A.G.G. got 16—and Mr. Wylie fared as badly as I, which consoled me somewhat!

The next morning 7 guns—the A.G.G., Mr. Evans, Major Hancock, Mr. Cruikshank, and Mr. Evans' brother, and myself—and someone else—went out after partridge and quail. We had a most enjoyable day, and obtained 125 head—partridge, black partridge, hares and quail. I got 4 hares, and 10 grey partridge. The only unfortunate incident was when we found ourselves trudging, late in the afternoon, across the roughest ploughed land I have ever encountered, which seemed to stretch for miles and miles in front of us. To judge from his language, the A.G.G. found it particularly trying—he was, unfortunately, only wearing rubber soled shoes, which were entirely unsuited to such rough going.

We ran out of cartridges, left the line, and cut across country to the cars.

I accompanied the A.G.G. to Kotah via Deoli and Bundi on the 14th December. The Guest House, situated on the banks of the Chambul, is most charming in every way.

H.H. the Mahorao took us for a drive that evening, during which we saw several large herds of black-buck. He asked me if I would like to shoot one, and as I had never shot a black-buck, I told him I should. The next morning the Maharao's private secretary called for me after breakfast. Expecting to have to stalk, I was dressed in a khaki shirt and shorts. however, we drove to within two hundred yards of this tame herd, and I was given a rifle. The buck showed only a perfunctory interest in me as I lay down and prepared to shoot. The rifle I had was a double-barrelled one, and the thought struck me that if I were to fire one barrel, the buck would afford me a running-shot with the second barrel. Since they were so tame, and there were so many small herds, it would not greatly matter if I missed one. Consequently, I fired one barrel. To my surprise, some five ran, but the remainder simply stood and watched me.

I singled out what appeared to be the best head, and shot the beast dead. The head proved to be 22 inches.

A day later, after breakfast, we saw a good-sized crocodile basking in the sun on the bank of a small island in the river, opposite the Guest House. The A.G.G. lent me a rifle, and in front of him, Lady Chetwode, and one of the Commander-in-Chief's A.D.C.s, Captain Coddrington of the Coldstream, I shot. The magar flopped into the water, and four days later was found. Unfortunately, it had been partially eaten, and the skin was useless.

One afternoon, as we were going up the Chambul river in H.H.'s launch, a bear scrambled up the bank on our approach. The A.G.G. shot twice at it, but the rocking of the boat was not conducive to good shooting, and the bear escaped unscathed.

A few months earlier, Col. Ogilvie had shot a fine tiger near the same place, under the same circumstances.

The A.G.G., Mrs. Ogilvie, Vere Birdwood and Sonia, and I, arrived in Udaipur on 24th December. Early on Christmas morning we motored out to Jaisamund, to join H.H. the Maharana's shooting-camp. The lake is most beautiful, and is, I am told, the second largest artificial lake in the world. In shape it roughly resembles a mushroom, with the "bund" at the end of the stalk. The Maharana's palace stands at one end, and the guest-house at the other end of the bund. There are several islands on the lake, and numerous hilly and well-wooded promontories jut out into it. The Maharana paid an official call, and gave us all Christmas presents—mine was a locally-made white metal cigarette-box—and we returned the call half-an-hour after his departure from the guest-house.

The next morning we set off on a panther-beat. H.H. the Maharana had a large party in his shikar-burj on the left of the line; the A.G.G. and another party was in the centre, and the remaining four of us were on the right in a small shooting-tower. It was very exciting to hear the cries of the beaters in the distance, and to see sounders of pig, monkeys, and hare come out of the jungle. A fine Sambhar came out and stood some fifty yards away from us, presenting an easy shot, but we waited for the panther, and so did not shoot it. Unfortunately, no panther appeared. Mr. Chevenix-Trench shot a pig, and H.H. the Maharana a Sambhar.

The following day a different stretch of jungle was beaten for panther. The A.G.G. with most of the party were stationed in a tower on top of the hill, while Amar Singh, Balkishen, and I sat on a quickly-constructed *machān* of stout rope, slung in the branches of a tree some way to the left rear of the tower.

From where we were, I had an excellent view of the panther coming over the hill. It lay near a mass of rock, when Col. Ogilvie fired at it and wounded the beast, which started down the hill in our direction.

Four shots were then fired from the tower, which killed the panther, a small female.

*   *   *   *   *

The A.G.G.'s visit to Jodhpur in 1934 afforded me my next opportunity for shooting. The guests of H.H. the Maharaja on that occasion included the polo team of the 10th Hussars, and the Jaipur team.

On the evening of the 13th January, some 50 of us left Jodhpur by special train for a duck shoot. We arrived the next morning at our destination, and breakfasted in a large marquee pitched beside the railway-line. From there we drove 23 miles to the tank. At 11 o'clock shooting commenced, and continued until 1 o'clock. The birds flew lower than they had at Bharatpur, and did not leave the tank. Twenty-five guns secured 800 head of duck. I bagged 21, including a pintail, and a red-crested pochard. The rest were teal and shoveller. My first butt had not proved very profitable by noon, so I waded out to an unoccupied butt in the centre of the tank for the remaining hour of shooting; far many more birds came over me in my new butt, and I enjoyed the shoot tremendously. H.H. the Maharaja of Jaipur bagged 70 birds.

On the 21st of January, the A.G.G., Mrs. Ogilvie and I went to Jaipur, to stay with H.H. the Maharaja·at Rambagh Palace, a most delightful place. The house-party left for Sawai Madhopur on the morning of the 25th, and arrived in time for lunch, leaving immediately afterwards for a tiger-beat.

My *machān* was on the extreme left of the line, and consequently I unfortunately saw nothing of the tiger, which appeared at the other end of the line, hidden from me by high ground and trees. However, the tiger apparently charged just below H.H. the Maharaja's *machān*. The Maharaja fired, and broke the tiger's near fore-leg. The beast continued on into the jungle, and was found and killed a quarter of a mile away by Khakur Bhairon Singh. It proved to be a 9ft. male, but was extremely heavy and fat.

The next morning we went on a "general beat". Owing to the largeness of the party, Major Kanwar Amar Singh (Comptroller of H.H.'s household) and I elected to sit on a rock on the right of the line, and not in a *machān*. Shortly after the beat commenced, a bear appeared sixty yards to our left, and opposite the A.G.G.'s *machān*. Col. Ogilvie fired and wounded it badly. It cried most piteously, until he fired again and killed it.

A hyaena came within ten yards of us, which Amar duly killed, and some Sambhar broke through the line unscathed down on the left flank.

That afternoon we set out on another tiger-beat, which proved fruitless. Rao Bahadur Jhakut Man Singh (a lad of 19, and known to his friends as "Rabbit") and I sat on a rock, and would have had a wonderful view had any tiger appeared.

We then held an impromptu beat by lining a roadway on our return journey. A small herd of Sambhar broke through, and the A.G.G. shot the male, but only wounded it. The Maharaja killed it with a beautiful shot.

We returned to Jaipur City that evening. Prior to leaving for Sawai Madhopur we had a short duck-shoot, which I omitted to mention. The bag was 160, of which I obtained only 7.

H.E. the Viceroy and Lady Willingdon visited Bikaner on the 23rd February 1934, to unveil the statue of the Maharaja erected by the citizens. The ceremony was interesting and impressive, and was followed by a State banquet, after which the party adjourned to the Fort for an Indian entertainment.

On the morning of the 25th February, the party left Lallgarh Palace by car for Gajner, and after lunch were stationed round Gajner Lake, Chaundasagar, Sugansagar, and Darbari Tanks for a duckshoot. There were 220 birds picked up, 160 of which were shot by the guns of Gajner. My butt was on the road skirting Chaundasagar, and very few birds came near me, and those that did were extremely high. Right at the end of the shoot, when I was in despair of ever hitting anything, I changed my butt, and within a minute brought down a very high pintail. On our particular tank, 5 guns shot only 15 birds.

The following morning we were installed into the many round butts for an Imperial Sand-grouse shoot. No less than 922 birds were picked up, but the individual bags were curiously varying, and were to a large extent dependent on the position of the butt. I collected 9 birds. H.E. the Viceroy had 70 head, H.H. the Maharaja 112, the Maharaj Kumar, Hiru, 118, Col. Ogilvie 50, and General Sir Charles McWatt 61. There were 26 guns.

From this shoot we went direct to Kidamdesar Tank to shoot Demoiselle Crane (Kunj). My butt was on His Highness' left, and I was one of the first arrivals. A flight of Kunj came over, and the Maharaj Kumar shouted out to me to shoot. I did so, and brought one down—the first of the day. Altogether, 115 of these birds were shot, to which total I contributed 12.

We again had an Imperial Sandgrouse shoot on the 27th, after which 670 birds were picked up. The individual bags varied from 80 to 2, and I was 17th out of 26 guns with 8 birds. The Viceroy's was the highest individual score.

We left Bikaner on the 27th evening, after a most delightful time.

The A.G.G., Mr. Lothian (Resident in Jaipur) and I motored from Ajmer to Kishangarh after luncheon on the 11th March. After taking tea with H.H. the Maharaja, he took us out pig-shooting. I was lent a small rifle for the occasion. Each of us, the three visitors, secured two boars, though none was particularly large.

The A.G.G., Mrs. Ogilvie and I moved to Mount Abu on the 15th March, arriving at the Residency early on the 16th. On the 21st morning, H.H. the Maharao of Sirohi motored Col. Ogilvie and me to Sirohi, arriving in time for luncheon. Colonel Ogilvie was asked if he would like to sit up for a panther that evening, but declined, and proposed that I might take his place.

I accordingly left the Guest House, accompanied by two Shikaris, father and son, at 5.30 p.m. that evening. A *machān* had been constructed on the ground, by means of cutting a corner out of a large cactus bush and fencing it in with a wickerwork frame of leaves and twigs.

The younger shikari and I sat there on "muda" chairs, and waited patiently. At 7.50 we heard an hyaena braying, and the shikari whispered something, and switched on the torch. A female panther was lying about five yards from the live goat which had been tethered to a stump some 20 yards in front of the *machān*. I was quite unprepared, and had no idea that the man was going to switch on the torch so quickly. I hastily took aim, but the panther bounded first to the other side of the goat, and then straight at us. It swerved aside just in front of the *machān* and I fired. However, no blood was found on the ground, and I returned, rather despondently, to dinner.

The next morning, before I was up, the Shikari arrived with the dead panther. My bullet had taken it in the shoulder, and passed obliquely through the body, leaving a large exit-hole. She measured 6ft.

Just before luncheon that day, Mr. Laird MacGregor, I.C.S., the Chief Minister of the State, asked me if I would like to go out again, since there was "khabar" of another panther, and the A.G.G. had again declined. I jumped at the chance, and Mrs. Langlands, who had come over from Erinpura with her husband, Major Langlands, 8th Gurkhas, who was then commanding the detachment of the Mina Corps at Erinpura, asked if she might come with me.

We reached the *machān* at 6.15, and climbed into it. It was built in a large tree near the hills about 6 miles from Sirohi Town. We had been there exactly half-an-hour, and it was still daylight, when a female panther scampered out of the undergrowth, and as she was about to kill the tethered goat, I shot her. She rolled over, growled three times, and died.

I was about to clamber out of the *machān* when we distinctly heard another panther "calling". We decided to wait, in the hopes of getting another shot. Dusk fell, and we could still hear this "calling" at intervals. Then we heard the beast moving, but could see nothing. We distinctly heard the padding sound of him moving below us, and his grunting as he breathed. He remained for at least half-an-hour directly below our *machān*, and it occurred to me that perhaps the beast was stalking us! We sat absolutely motionless. Suddenly he bounded out towards the goat, and I took what aim I could in the dark. I could see the panther only with difficulty, and the foresight not at all. I then whispered to Mrs. Langlands to switch on the torch. As bad luck would have it, the battery was almost exhausted, so that it gave a wretched light, and the torch had not been focussed. Consequently, there was a faint outer rim of light, and darkness in the centre.

Mrs. Landlands tried to move the torch so that the light would be better, and I fired, unable still to see either the panther clearly or the foresight of the rifle. I found my bullet hole when we cautiously climbed down, and I thought, from its position, that I had hit the panther. Since the search-party next morning had a fruitless errand, I conclude that my bullets must have passed over the animal; in the dark I must have taken too much foresight—a very great pity.

The dead female panther measured 6ft.

On the 12th of April, Sirohi Vakil sent word that a cow had been killed, and partially eaten, by a panther near Oria dak bungalow and Captain Bedi kindly lent me his car to take me out. The remains of the cow were lying in a small nulllah about a mile from Oria, and I reached the place at 5.30 p.m. I sat in the *machān* until 8.30, but no panther appeared. Six mongooses enjoyed a hearty meal off the putrefying remains of the cow.

Early on the 17th April, information was brought in to Capt. Bedi that a cow had been killed near Anadra the previous night. Bedi kindly arranged for me to go to sit over the kill, and I left Abu on foot at 4 p.m. It was nearly six miles to the kill, right at the foot of the hills, and I did not reach the *machān* until 5.40 p.m. Shakūr, Capt. Bedi's shikari, and I climbed up into the *machān*, and waited there. I had expected an early appearance of the panther, but it grew dark and still he had not come. At 7.50 I was afraid that he would not materialise at all, when suddenly I saw a most indistinct shadow—ghostly in the very wan moonlight—flit across the cow's remains. I levelled my rifle, switched on the torch which was clamped on to the barrel, and saw a good sized male panther staring up at the light. My bullet hit him in the neck, and he dropped dead. He measured 7ft. 4ins., and was an old beast. Bedi, who has considerable experience of panthers in and around Abu, tells me that I cannot hope to shoot a larger panther in the vicinity.

The climb back up the hill was extremely tiring, but I was pleased to have shot my first male panther on my birthday.

On Sunday, April 22nd, Daya (Capt. D. S. Bedi) and I were out at 6 o'clock in the morning, beyond "Sunset Point", in the optimistic hope of seeing something to shoot. It was a beautiful morning and we sat on the hillside for over an hour. Soon after 7 o'clock we saw a bear about 800 yards away, right down in the nullah. He was out of range—effective range, at all events—and was soon out of sight. We returned to breakfast, and left immediately afterwards for a place in which another bear had been reported. We ensconsed ourselves on a large rock, and the beat began—we had but 10 beaters. Unfortunately, the bear broke cover some 200 yards above us, moving fast across our front. The enormous boulders and undergrowth prevented us seeing him clearly for any length of time. We both took snap shots at him, but both missed. In extenuation, I can honestly say that it was extremely difficult shooting!

That evening we went out to inspect a tiger "kill". It was in a difficult place, and none of us had any hope that the tiger—the notorious old rogue, who has done so much damage round here—would return, and so we walked back to Abu.

At 6 p.m. on April the 29th I was walking back from Trevol Tal, where I spent a pleasant day bathing and picnicking. Mrs. Lothian suddenly came along in the Residency car, and said that a villager had come in with khabar of a tiger kill. I returned in the car, changed into shikar kit, borrowed the A.G.G.'s rifle and torch, and set off in the car to Abu High School. From there I went on foot to the left of the School to the "kill", some 1½ miles distant.

The tiger had killed two buffaloes the night before, and the carcasses were lying about 100 yards apart, in a densely wooded nullah. A *machān* had been erected over each "kill", but I chose the one lower down the slope, since it seemed to me that if he came at all—and I was very doubtful, since it was obviously our old friend, the wily rogue whose reputation was that he never returned to a kill—he would come up from below, and not visit the higher buffalo first. The *machān* was really too low for my liking; the bottom of it was but a meagre 10ft. above the ground, but no more convenient place for the *machān* was apparent, and so I decided to sit there. I had with me one of our chuprassis, Fazal, who was unarmed. We were quietly sitting in the *machān* at 7 p.m. I had no great hope, then, that the tiger would appear, and was just wondering how long it would be worthwhile sitting in that extremely restricted and cramped *machān*, when noiselessly an enormous tiger appeared like a white wraith on a small track immediately in front of us. To my inexperienced eye he seemed truly gigantic. The very dim half-light aided the illusion, of course, since although there was a full moon, very little light percolated through the heavy undergrowth. The tiger stared up at the *machān*, standing motionless 25 yards away. I sat and watched him, not moving a muscle. He decided that there was nothing to fear from that quarter, and turned his head to his right. I seized the opportunity to put the muzzle of the rifle, with the electric torch clamped on to it, through the small aperture in the *machān*. The tiger slowly came forward, with head down, and when he was well out in the open clearing, I aimed, switched on the torch, and fired. When the slight smoke from the muzzle had cleared, I saw that he was still standing, obviously badly wounded, and roaring feebly. I decided that another shot could do no harm, in case he was but temporarily disabled, and fired again. He fell, and rolled down the slight slope out of sight, his roaring stopped, and all was quiet. We waited for 10 minutes—it was 7.30 when I fired first—and then called up the villagers who had been waiting half a mile away. I then climbed down from the *machān*, and with rifle ready, approached the bushes into which he had rolled. There he was, stretched out in the undergrowth. The villagers threw stones at him, and as he showed no signs of life, went up to the beast. My bullets were within six inches of each other, at the base of the neck, and had entered from above. The first shot had been quite sufficient to kill him. Carried by a mob of villagers, and slung on stout poles, the tiger arrived at the Residency at 2 a.m. The next morning most of the inhabitants of Abu arrived to view the animal, the first tiger shot in this vicinity in Major Tarbotton's memory, which extends over the last 12 years, although this beast, which is, I am told, at least 10 years old, had been ravaging the countryside, abetted by his mate and cubs, for the last five years. The tiger measured 9 foot 4 inches, and was immensely broad, with abnormally powerful shoulders and legs—due, I presume, to the hilly nature of the country.

I can only add that this incident furnishes an excellent example of "beginner's luck"!'

'*Later*—Khan Bahadur Modi, who has resided in Abu for many years, and who is a noted shikari, tells me that this is the first tiger shot near Abu for 20 years, the third within 45 years, and the largest of those three.'

Chapter Four

THE HIGH HILLS OF LADAKH—1940

'Every bridge that he makes
Either buckles or breaks . . .'

It was a bitter disappointment to Leslie Fry to be refused permission time and time again to return to the Army from the Indian Political Service in 1939. Although he accepted the reasons for the authorities' refusal as logical enough, in a time of war in Europe when his own posting had a specialised function that applied as much then as before, he could not quell his soldier's instinct to be at the hub of the war. He was also pursued by a sense of isolation, and found it frustrating to be unable to make any obvious contribution to Britain's and the Allies' stand.

The fact was that he had been in the I.P.S. for six years and was an increasingly valuable, experienced member of a service whose small numbers—unlikely to be increased in a time of war—were subject to the natural decrease resulting from retirement and the sickness and mortality that took more than an average toll of the men, who worked in an alien climate at the pace set by an energetic administration.

It was perhaps to put an end to Leslie's repeated requests for transfer back into military life and the scene of action, that he was posted early in 1940 to Jammu and Kashmir State as Under Secretary to the Resident and—as he deemed the more important part of the assignment—British Joint Commissioner in Ladakh. Among his responsibilities was the superintendence of the Central Asia Treaty Road, a sonorous name for the track which ran through the Himalayas from Gagangir, some 45 miles from Srinagar, up to the Karakoram Pass into Chinese Turkestan.

Ladakh itself is the eastern part of the State, and in earlier times was known as Little or Western Tibet. During the Sikh wars it had been annexed by Gulab Singh, the Maharaja of Jammu. By remaining benevolently neutral on the British right flank he had then contributed to the defeat of the Sikhs, then bought the prize spoil of Kashmir from the victors. He and his heirs thus became Maharajas of Jammu and Kashmir.

On the 27th May 1940, equipped with two Union Jacks (one large, one small), as it was an exercise in part to show the flag, Leslie set out from Srinagar for a destination 250 miles to the east. His train consisted of a senior Muslim official from the British Residency who knew the area they were to cover, a clerk, and the usual assortment of personal servants.

They travelled on ponies of mixed breed, shaggy aspect, and indomitable stamina. With them they carried their stores, and gifts for the notables they would meet on their tour.

They were to return on the 27th August of the same year, and no British successor in the I.P.S. was ever to visit Leh, the capital of Ladakh, again. The current presence of the Communists and the exile of the Lamaseries after the war meant that Leslie saw a Tibet that was never to be the same. But it is characteristic of him that he framed his duties in Kipling's words from Potophar Gubbins, C.E.: 'Every bridge that he makes either buckles or breaks'. What he was really doing was a tour of inspection, in which he had to arrange for repairs needed on the road and the bridges of their route with local contractors, and see that the work was carried through, but being Leslie—with his enquiring mind and appetite for new places—he added to this by producing a detailed diary of impressions that will always be of interest as a social document. He himself saw it as very much the product of a young man's mind, but was not ashamed to admit that the same time as writing it he was reading Pepys, and the diarist's habit was catching! In fact in Pepys he found some comfort . . . Pepys constantly expected ruin and massacre, not to mention defeat, to come of the Carlovingian wars of his time. He was wrong. Interspersed among the chronicle of the Ladakh days are many of Leslie's own comments on the progress of the battle he was unable to join, and they are characteristically aware of, and in judgment of, the other fellows' application of 'sauve qui peut'.

The edited version of the Diary that follows has been cut on the lines that Leslie Fry himself indicated when planning the final text of his autobiography . . .

'The official guide-book says that the first stage or so of the journey from Srinagar to Leh can be done by tonga; those days (Alhamdul 'illah!) are gone, and it now possible to cover the first forty-four miles by car. The road proved however rather more difficult than we had expected, and to make matters worse the car unaccountably developed some defect in the petrol-supply system. We left Srinagar at 10 a.m. on the 27th May, but did not reach Gagangir, the end of the motorable part of the road, until 1.30 p.m.

My track from then on ran along the Sing valley, with jagged hills, well wooded on the lower slopes, on either side. The stream is shallow, very tortuous, muddy and fast flowing. After five and a half miles of easy and interesting walking the hills opened out into a grass plateau, almost unnaturally green, at the far end of which the track turned east into a small second plain: the 'marg' which gives the tiny village of Sonamarg its name. Ghulam Rasul had led my pony behind me (probably wondering why on earth I didn't ride) from Gagangir, and since it is not fitting for the British Joint Commissioner to arrive at a Camp on foot I mounted a quarter of a mile from the Camp and rode in. The pony, incidentally, is a placid bay with a shambling gait and a peculiar trot; what there is left of the mounted Cavalry have a name for it, implying "disjointed".

My tent, a 180 pounder, was pitched on the grass bank of the stream—an ideal spot. The Union Jack, charged with the Star of India, which was run up outside the tent as I dismounted, seemed a trifle vainglorious. But if the main purpose of the trip is my Government's prestige the flag is clearly necessary. I confess it gave me a thrill of pleasure, as, in fact, it always does anywhere, but never more than outside my tent for the first time.

Sultan, my Kashmiri cook engaged for the tour, had left Srinagar with the heavy kit on the 25th and so had tea and a bath ready for me at Sonamarg. The coolies had ensconced themselves close up against the hillside and were cooking a meal; they seem a cheery lot, and explained their arrangements for the night with a good deal of amusement. The ponies had been stabled in the Serai, a dingy, badly built place with grass sprouting from its mud roofs.

The higher of the hills around the marg are still covered in snow. The smallest hill, immediately behind my tent, is densely wooded with tall dark firs and some shorter trees with light green foliage; the contrast between the greens is charming. Away to the south east lie very much more formidable hills. Altogether, this is a most delightful camp site.

The inevitable chicken was produced for dinner, though this one was less tough than most. In any case (and I am, at a conservative estimate, the three millionth person to have made this observation on trek in Kashmir) food always tastes better in the open. I slept extremely well.

Jeeves called me at 7, and by 9 o'clock Camp had been struck and the baggage train was on the march. I remained behind because by pre-arrangement Bill Robertson-Taylor (?) was to leave Srinagar by dawn and join me. I occupied my time in climbing the wooded hill behind my camp and found that its charm at close quarters was even greater, enhanced as the dark firs were by clusters of wild flowers, irises a foot high, and short, white upright flowers like crocuses. It was stupid of me not to bring a book on the trees and flowers likely to be met with in Kashmir.

R.T. joined me before noon. The nine miles from Sonamarg to Baltal runs through pastureland and patches of wooded country, an easy and pleasant march which we accomplished in three hours, R.T. by pony and I on foot, though I rode the last quarter of a mile into camp. Again we have a charming site, in the angle where the main Sind River is joined by a mountain stream tumbling down from the North East. The celebrated cave of Amarnath—to many Hindus almost what Mecca is to all Muslims—is farther up the main stream, too far to be reached without devoting a day to it, which I cannot easily afford to do. It is sacred to Siva, who is said to have taken up his abode there in the form of a block of ice; thousands of pilgrims visit the cave every year.

Incidentally, the only traveller met to-day was a Mr. Wallace W. Kirkland, an American journalist on the staff of *Life*, who photographed my baggage train and took a couple of snapshots of me, whether for publication (as he said) or whether because he thought it was expected of him was difficult to say, but I imagine the latter.

Early to bed, as we tackle the Zojiha to-morrow. Our present camp at Baltal is some 9,000 feet above sea level and the top of the pass is another 2,500 feet higher. The road appears from here very steep and difficult, and I understand that we shall have to cross a certain amount of snow.

The heavy kit left camp this morning, the 29th May; R.T. and I were called at 4.30—and very cold it was too—and began the ascent at 5.10. In winter the route through the pass runs along the bottom of the ravine, but the snow-bed melts in the Spring and the zigzag path up the mountain-side must then be followed. I began by riding half a mile, but my feet became so numbed with cold that I took to walking. The gradient was in fact slight and as a climb the ascent cannot be compared with any of the Waziristan hills up which I have so often led a piquet. There was a good deal of snow on the top pass, treacherously soft in places, and it seemed to be that our journey was begun either too early or too late: too early because in a short time the snow will have disappeared, or too late because hitherto the snow must have been frozen hard and so easier to walk on. The crossing was however accomplished without mishap. Once beyond the pass (I find from the guide-book that it is only 11,300 feet above sea level) the route debouches into a narrow, level valley of about a quarter of a mile in width, very gradually descending into Baltistan. The change in height is imperceptible.

We reached Machoi (sometimes spelt Mitsahoi), about nine miles from Baltal, just before 9 a.m. and sat on the dak bungalow verandah to have breakfast of coffee, hard boiled eggs, and biscuits. I had walked eight and a half of the nine miles but felt no ill-effects whatsoever, either from the height, snow or ascent. My chappals were however wet through and I changed into shoes. The Machoi Serai and Dak Bungalow are the first (from Srinagar) of those on the Treaty Road in my charge as British Joint Commissioner, and had to be inspected.

The second part of the day's march, some six miles to Matayan, lay through comparatively uninteresting and uninspiring country. Patches of snow lay across parts of the route and the hills on either side of the narrow valley were covered in snow, miniature glaciers reaching down re-entrants to the valley. The Mininarg bridge had been heightened and strengthened during the past year, and had to be inspected.

We reached Matayan at exactly 12 noon. The Dak Bungalow is built on the far side of the village above the river, but the site is very different from the charming ones we had camped on at Sonamarg and Baltan. The hills around are devoid of vegetation and the ground is stony, and why the handful of families that inhabit the village should attempt to survive in this barren spot is beyond comprehension. The people of Matayan are without exception the poorest, dirtiest and most illiterate I have met with. The village consists of some dozen mud and stone huts vaguely resembling the villages of the N.W. Frontier but without the characteristic Pathan towers.

I was shown with some pride the only object of any interest in the village, a water-mill. A hollowed-out tree trunk carries water from a narrow channel down to a cavity below and turns a small wheel, which in turn operates a grinding-stone fed with grain from a wicker basket tilted at an angle and fixed to the ceiling of a room no more than four feet square, in which an old woman was crouching when I peered in. The only redeeming feature of the village is the river, without which the place would be a veritable Gehenna, a glimpse of Hell.

The march to Dras on the 30th May was a short one of twelve miles, about nine of which I did on foot. The route was easy and pleasant, following for the main part the river, a narrow, swift-flowing grey stream strewn with large boulders. The sky was intensely blue and cloudless, and the sun strong, as the state of my knees (I was wearing shorts) and arms testified by the time we reached camp at about 12.45; we had taken 3¾ hours on the journey, including halts. What appeared to be the entire population of Dras turned out to meet us, the school children lined up to intone a song of welcome. Our camp site is on a pleasant stretch of grass lined with willow trees, and the village seems far more prosperous than the wretched Matayan.

Breakfast (at 6.30) on the 31st was not a very happy affair, since neither the bacon nor the sausages we had brought with us had stood up to the journey very well and we found them uneatable. We left Dras at 7.30 and had soon left the open, grassy valley behind. Were it not for the Dras river, which the road follows for the whole of the march, one might well imagine oneself in Waziristan; the hills rise to a considerable height on either side of the river and are completely barren, giving a depressing feeling of desolation. Having put my walking muscles into good order I had decided to ride most of this march, and had consequently put on breeches; the breeches in question had been made for me when I went to the R.M.C. fourteen years ago, and being a "uniform" pattern had not been worn a great deal since . . . certainly not since I transferred to the Political. Either the breeches had shrunk or my knees become larger—at all events I soon found that both walking and riding were most uncomfortable, and though I managed, by judiciously combining both, to last out for sixteen miles, I had to change into shorts during our lunch-time halt.

We reached Kharbu at 2.30; seven hours taken on twenty-two odd miles, including a twenty minutes' talk with the Wazir of Ladakh (who is also my Joint Commissioner for this part of the road) and a thirty minutes' halt for lunch, was a good timing. Owing to my unsatisfactory breeches I had covered something like fifteen miles on foot and only seven on horseback, which possibly was just as well, since it is unwise to attempt to "condition" oneself too rapidly to riding when one has not been in the saddle for some time; my camp clerk, who gaily rode the first two marches, is now unable to ride at all and has to trudge along the whole of each march.

My tent at Kharbu was pitched in a small plantation of willows, apparently the only trees that will grow in the place; the site is 11,890 feet above sea level, the highest point we have yet reached, not excluding the Zojiha. R.T., who has "a heart", is fortunately not showing signs of it. Certain of the local inhabitants at every stage have however come to me with their ailments, for which I have unfailingly prescribed and administered a couple of the "Constipation Pills" (as the bottle is labelled) from the chest of medicines provided for me by the Residency Surgeon, George Ledgard. This treatment can at all events do no harm and is, in the majority of cases, probably quite correct. As for me, I am extremely fit though uncomfortably sunburnt about the chin and knees.

Our march on the 1st June was a short one of fifteen miles, to Kargil, capital of the Purig District. The route tended to be wearisome, through barren hills unrelieved by cultivation or villages. Shortly after Kharbu the river joins the Dras, and later on the Suru flows into the same stream. For the last six miles to Kargil the road follows the Suru valley until it opens out into the wide but uneven plain upon which several hamlets stand, the biggest being Kargil itself.

The stretch of river below Kargil bazar is the most turbulent I have ever seen, the water (very muddy at this time of year) rushing down with great force over the large boulders in the river-bed and producing the effect of a rough sea.

The Dak bungalow stands on the far side of the main village, and is the best we have met with so far on the Treaty Road; its compound did not, however, afford a suitable camping-ground, so I stayed in the bungalow itself.

The war has seemed very far away since we have been away from civilisation, but at these occasional stops that we make, news does seep through in the way of rather out-dated newspapers delivered with the inevitable packet of official correspondence. The incredible news of the capitulation of the Belgian Army at King Leopold's command reached us here at Kargil. Although we cannot judge Leopold, history will never forgive him for not informing his Allies of his decision before putting it into effect, if only to give them time and opportunity to withdraw. As it was, the B.E.F. and part of the French army, surrounded on three sides and with an outlet only to Dunkirk, have had to be evacuated, an operation of exceptional difficulty which appears to have been magnificently handled.

It is of course rash to attempt to prophesy, but it seems to me that this very serious reverse may prove to be a blessing in disguise. In Flanders the B.E.F. and the French were fighting to protect the Channel ports, advantages of occupying which, without command of the sea, seem doubtful, for the few extra miles so gained by the German Air Force can mean little in these days of long-distance flights. With our Armies withdrawn unbeaten in the field and re-formed, we have at our disposal a striking-force for use where we will when the moment for our counter-attack comes. There is certainly no need for pessimism, and my conviction in our ultimate success is unshaken.

We were visited shortly after tea by Messrs. Reid, Mazzoni and Berger (the first an Englishman and the others French-Swiss) of the Central Asian Mission, who stayed with us until almost dinner time.

Sunday, the 2nd June, was spent in Kargil for a variety of reasons; we needed a rest; the town is the biggest between Srinagar and Leh and so merits attention; and because the Treaty Road runs through the large bazar several unusual repairs to it were required and had to be inspected before being sanctioned. I spent the morning in inspecting the Dak bungalow and Serai with the Sub-Overseer responsible for their maintenance, and in dealing with correspondence, files, and a few complaints by the Treaty Road carriers against local shopkeepers. The afternoon was spent in the bazar; its most obvious need is a drain, which I promptly ordered.

The march of 23 miles from Kargil to Mulbek is the longest of the whole journey, and took us from 8.15 to 3 p.m. on the 3rd June. The road crosses three or four miles of barren, stony plain, the Thangskam, and then descends to Paskyum, a fertile village on the banks of the Wakka stream. For the next twelve miles the route follows a narrow gorge and is monotonous though not difficult. Shargol, eighteen miles from Kargil, marks the beginning of the Buddhist country, though a sprinkling of Mohammedans is still to be found beyond; Buddhism was restored in this part of the world after being suppressed by the Modammedan ruler of Skardu. Monasteries are a feature of the landscape, perching above each village, and along the route, always outside a village and frequently at intermediate points, are long, built-up heaps of stone covered with flat stones carved with holy inscriptions; R.T. has already proclaimed his intention of removing a suitable specimen on his way back, an act of desecration I shall probably emulate. At these heaps of stone, which are called Mani walls, the path invariably divides so that the traveller can pass the heap on his right. Another religious edifice very often met with is the Churten, a small, round cairn.

At Mulbek we were greeted by groups of women offering us bowls of coarse flour (which they by no means expected us to take) in return for alms. Massed on an open space in front of the Dak Bungalow was a larger force of women, two bands, and, a little apart, were five Lamas from the monastery, to all of whom I distributed cash in accordance with custom. The Buddhist dress must await description until I am more familiar with it. The open space, incidentally, is apparently the village polo-ground, but our arrival was too late to permit a game to be arranged for our benefit, and in any case my tent and flagstaff were already pitched in the middle of the ground.

Mulbek is 10,290 feet above sea level, a dirty village of no particular interest. Just beyond it, however, stands a carved idol 18 to 20 feet high, possessing four arms and hands, apparently a representation of Chamba.

From Mulbek the road rises to an easy pass, the Namika La, 13,000 feet above sea level, with an equally easy descent on the other side. Bodh Kharbu, our next halting place, is 11,890 feet above sea level, on the Sangeloomah stream which eventually falls into the Indus; the march of fifteen miles from Mulbek was easy and pleasant. We were again met by parties of women, bands and Lamas, to whom the inevitable distribution of largesses had to be made; I fortunately receive a special grant from Government on this account.

We left Bodh Kharbu at 8 a.m. and reached Lamayuru, our next halting place, at 1.15. The only difficult part of this fifteen mile march was the Foti La, a pass of 13,400, which I crossed on foot; in fact, I walked fourteen of the total fifteen miles.

The view from the top of the pass was very extensive, range after range of hills (the highest hill still covered with snow) stretching out on all sides, but was to some extent detracted from by the cloudiness of the day and consequent bad visibility. What we lost in the view however we gained in comfort, for the march is, I understand, usually hot and tiring, whereas we found it almost too cold.

The descent beyond the pass was steeper than the ascent up to it (I shall not make the return crossing on foot) and brought us down into the valley which, after an ascending turn, opens out into the basin in which Lamayuru stands. This sudden view is by far the most picturesque we have so far met with; at one moment we were climbing a short slope in the barren valley, and the next we saw, stretching down the hill side, tier below tier, the quaint buildings of Lamayuru, descending into green fields and trees on the river bank. The whole effect is unworld-like, certainly un-Indian (indeed, it is Thibetan), and bizarre.

As usual, we were welcomed by Lamas, bands, groups of women, school children drawn up into two ranks. The school master, after announcing "Three cheers for the honourable (an addition of his own) British Joint Commissioner", proceeded to call for only two! Then dozens of small posies of wild roses and irises were pressed into my hand and there seemed a general air of cheerfulness about the village.

Cheerfulness seems to be the most obvious characteristic of these simple people (apart, I almost omitted to mention, from their more obvious dirtiness); it is difficult for us to imagine what they have to be cheerful about; they are born, they live, they have their being, and they die; their lot is hard, an unending struggle against Nature, and I can only suppose that their happiness comes from an entire lack of civilisation as we know it.

Leaving Lamayuru at 8 a.m. on the 6th June we dropped into a narrow, tortuous gorge which the path (I should say, the Treaty Road) follows for some five or six miles, emerging first into a wider valley and then, ten miles from Lamayuru, into the Khaltse plateau. The greenness of the Moravian Mission garden in Khaltse village was welcome after the barrenness of the gorge, and we halted at the Dak Bungalow at 11.30 for lunch; I had in any case to inspect the bungalow's state of repair and furniture. Here again we were given the usual welcome and distributed small presents of money.

Leaving Khaltse at 12.30 we covered the level but stony seven miles to Nurla by 2.30, and once more were received by women, bands, and school children. Nurla, a plateau between steep, bare hills, is very green at this time of year, and our camp, situated in a grove of apricot trees (surely unusual at 10,000 feet above sea level?) is one of the pleasantest we have had.

After a monotonous march from Nurla to Saspul on the 7th June, with R.T. doing more and more walking and less and less riding, we were on the last lap of our outward journey to Leh. At 10.30 on the 8th June we reached Bazgo, a large picturesque village, and three miles further on we came to Nimu, where the Zanskar river joins the Indus. The march was uninteresting, and had it not been for the cloudy sky would have been hot. The Rev. Mr. Ferguson, a member of the Church Missionary Society from Agra, arrived some hours after us and dined with us. He is spending his leave walking to Leh and back, from Srinagar.

Our march on the 9th was only to Spitak, a distance of thirteen miles, although Leh itself is only five miles further. The reason for this apparently unnecessary halt seems to be to allow the B.J.C to collect himself and his train for their entry into Leh. The march was uninteresting, for the most part across a stony, sterile plain, and we were glad to drop down to the Indus valley and the green oasis of the village. We were welcomed by Mr. Gautama, Special Charas Officer, Leh; the Naib Tahsildar; and the Arsakal. Captain Hira Singh, commanding the Leh garrison, arrived later.

The gentlemen who awaited me at Spitak yesterday returned this morning, the 10th, to escort me to Leh. The cavalcade was swollen by the Raja of Ladakh, the Gyal-Po—or "priest-king"—(cf. Carlyle, "On Heroes and Hero-worship"), the Rev. Driver, a Moravian missionary from Leh, and sundry Central Asian traders and shopkeepers of Leh. The chuprassis wore their scarlet coats and rode ahead of the main body, but the sum was, I fear, that of a party of Chinese Irregular Cavalry. However, it was a glorious morning and everyone seemed very cheerful, and we covered the five miles in an hour and a quarter.

Leh seems less a town than the nucleus of several villages straggling over a wide, green plateau bounded on three sides by barren hills behind which rise snow-covered peaks. Prominent on a hill to the East of the town is the old and now disused palace of the Raja of Ladakh, who prefers to live in his jagir of Stok, eight miles to the South East of Leh. Expecting something much more imposing, we were disappointed with our first sight of Leh, but we shall probably find cause to modify this first impression as we get to know the place better.

A guard of honour of a platoon, detailed from the Company of the 6th Jammu and Kashmir Infantry at present on duty in Leh, was drawn up in the main street of the town and gave a General Salute when I arrived. Streamers inscribed "Welcome" were stretched from upper storey to upper storey at several places across the road and many houses had been decorated with flags; the streets were lined with sight-seers and more garlands were placed round my neck than I could conveniently manage. All the more important personages of the town fell in behind the procession as we surged along on foot, preceded by small boys, towards the Residency, where a small informal Darbar was held on the verandah while a dance was performed by a party of women on the lawn in front of the house.

The house is a square, double-storied, whitewashed building standing in about five acres of ground; its most notable feature, externally, is the verandah, which is supported by four wooden pillars, painted green, the wide tops of which are carved and painted in blues, reds and greens in a floral design, with here and there a Tibetan dragon's head. The view from the front of the house is very charming, down a stretch of grass lined with trees to the end of the compound and then down over the gradual descent to the Indus valley, five miles away, with the hills beyond, those to the left still covered in snow.

Our first task here was to install the wireless set kindly left behind for my use by the Rev. W. Asboe, Superintendent of the Moravian Mission, who has gone away on leave. The six-volt battery I brought up from Srinagar seemed no worse for the journey and the set functioned well. Jeeves and Faiz (R.T.'s bearer) soon had our kit unpacked and the house in order, and Sultan, the cook, appeared delighted to have a well-appointed kitchen to work in after the shifts and expediences of camp cooking; if not in the first flight of cooks, he is supremely cheerful even in the most adverse circumstances and is capable of producing a very reasonable meal after jogging twenty miles on a pony. Jeeves, Faiz, and Sultan stood the journey very creditably, though not even the toughest and most dangerous parts of the road, above yawning chasms, could make them dismount. The "Household Cavalry" remained firmly on their ponies, which must have been as glad as we were to arrive in Leh.

On the morning of the 11th I walked down to the Fort with R.T. and the Khan Sahib to inspect the garrison at the invitation of Captain Hira Hand, commanding the Company. The men are all Dogras, and seem smart and keen. The Fort itself was well kept and clean, and the barrack rooms in very good order. A good deal of building debris lying about inside the walls needs to be cleared away, but that is not my affair, and as my inspection was not a military, or even an official, one I could hardly comment on it. The new drill, in "threes"—instead of "fours"— seems to make for easier tactical handling (or manoeuvrability to use a newly-coined word) but not for smartness, though efficiency must of course come first.

After receiving a succession of visitors for short interviews on the 12th, we left Leh at 8 a.m. on the 13th, the war news that had in the meantime reached us becoming steadily worse. Italy's entry into the war, however, I do not feel need cause us alarm; if anything it is a further assurance (if one were needed) of our ultimate victory.

Our destination on the 13th was Hemis, for the annual festival at the Hemis Lamasery. This is the largest and most celebrated monastery in Ladakh, and the only one that escaped the attentions of Zorawar Singh, Maharaja Gulab Singh of Jammu's general. Two miles from Hemis, which was a seven hour march in all, we were met by the General Manager (for want of a better title) of the Lamasery; the Head Lama, or Skushog, died last year and no re-incarnation of him has yet been discovered. The Manager led us up the steep, winding path into a narrow re-entrant at the top of which the Lamasery is built, hidden from the Indus valley below, and saw us installed in our tents, which had been pitched in a very pleasant garden.

A Lama came at 8.30 on the 14th to bid us to the play, and first we were conducted up the steep path from our camp to the Lamasery, where the Manager was waiting to show us over parts of the building. The monastery proper is four storeys high, verandahs surmounted by valances running across the upper ones, and is built close up against the brown hills. A wide flight of steps leads up to the main entrance from the courtyard, and the big wooden doors at the top open into the main temple, which also serves, it appeared, as a dressing-room for the performers taking part in the play. The atmosphere in the temple was almost over-poweringly musty, and dust and dirt abounded; the gilt idols and hanging tapestries could barely be seen in the semi-darkness, and we found little to interest us in any of the four or five rooms we were shown. It seems that all the Lamasery's valuables have been locked up until a new Skushog is appointed, and all that is left in use or on view is tawdry and cheap.

We were glad to get out into the fresh air and sunlight of the courtyard, around which squatted the spectators who had been patiently waiting for hours for the show to begin. In the middle of the courtyard, some ten yards apart from each other, were two flagstaffs almost as high as the monastery, topped by yaks' tails and swathed in long prayer flags. Above the monastery's main entrance had been hung a silk banner on which was painted a god with the traditional Buddha-type face. The box to which we were escorted was a closed-in, narrow verandah on the first floor of the building opposite the Lamasery, from which we looked down into the courtyard, where an entertainment was to be presented for our benefit. As we left the performance, a young Ladakhi woman in the crowd rushed past us down the steep slope that led from the monastery, and fell headlong. My man Jeeves aired his English with a well-aimed comment: "Too much drink, I think!".

We left Hemis at 8 a.m. on the 16th June and reached Leh at 3.45 p.m. Waiting for us was the news that Paris had been handed over to the Germans without opposition. I find this unaccountable. The city is not easily defended, and there is little point in subjecting it to devastation, but I fear the moral effect of its loss. Paris to the Frenchman is France. I am reading Pepys' diary again. It is comforting to see how often he expected defeat, ruin and massacre in our wars, only to have his expectations unfulfilled.

On the 18th we heard the amazing news that the French Government had asked for peace terms, and that the British Government had offered France a pact of union. To an Englishman the better course is obvious, but whether the French view the position in quite the same light is doubtful. Their losses in men and materials must have been enormous, and their retreat, so far from having been in good order, as the wireless and newspapers assure us, must latterly have been no better than a rout. "Sauve qui peut" and "la trahison" have, I suspect, been the phrases most commonly heard in France in the last few days. It is at present impossible to conjecture why the French poured money like water into the Maginot line without extending it to the sea, or why they permitted, apparently without counter attacking, the salient made at Sedan to be widened into an unbridgeable gulf through which the endless stream of German fighting vehicles has passed into the heart of France. The French say they will accept no dishonourable terms, but in suing for peace on any terms, in disregard of their treaty obligations to Great Britain, the corner-stone of their Temple of Honour has, it seems to me, crumbled—and soon nothing will be left.'

*   *   *   *   *

'The Raja of Ladakh, who was present at the Hemis festival, had invited us to visit him at Stok on the 20th. We left Leh at 9 a.m., and were met by the Raja and a mounted servant some four miles out of the town. He led us at a smart jog-trot (very good for the liver) across the stony plain down to the Indus valley and up the other side to his jagir; the nine miles took us exactly two hours.

The castle is built to the west of the village and, like most castles, is on a hill. To ascend the hill we had to dismount. The Rani met us very graciously in the courtyard, and presented me with a scarf of honour, which I put on.

We were then led into what I took to be the best sitting room, in one corner of which stood a private shrine. Against the far wall were two raised dais, one higher than the other, covered with strips of Yarkandi carpet and with low Lhasa tables before them. I unconsciously but (as I later learned) correctly took my seat cross-legged on the higher dais; R.T. sat on the other, but not cross-legged, while the Raja, Rani and their two sons, one aged 10 and the other 8, sat on carpets against the right-hand wall, tucking their crossed legs well under them. I have since discovered that to show the soles of one's feet, in any circumstances, is a gross breach of good manners in this part of the world. To stick one's tongue out is, on the contrary, a deferential greeting among Tibetans, though so far I have not noticed it practised in Ladakh.

The Raja is an amiable, vague man of about 45 or so, the Rani a pleasant forceful character perhaps a little younger; she comes of a Kulu family, and has applied herself to running the estate and retrieving the Raja's fortunes to some purpose. The Raja's father, who could never bring himself to recover his due revenue from his peasants, got heavily into debt, but at the instance of the B.J.C. and Residence of the time (1907) the Kashmir Government granted him an annual sum of Rs.5000, and the present Raja is comfortably, though not well, off. The father is still alive, living in retirement in Hemis, where indeed the present Raja's second daughter has also immured herself in religious study.

Conversation tended to flag. The Raja speaks Urdu but is far from communicative, while the Rani speaks nothing but Buddhi, of which I of course have no knowledge. We were brought cups of Ladakhi tea, with pats of butter swimming in them, but though the smell could be braved a sip was sufficient to induce a feeling of queasiness. The Raja and his family withdrawing, we got Jaraf Ali, my head chuprassi, to pour the tea into a large bowl and remove it; he seemed to think this a very understandable wish, but as he was walking away with the bowl of unwanted tea the Raja unfortunately returned but, if he noticed what was happening, made no comment.

We were then taken on to the roof of the castle, where we had a magnificent view over the Indus valley. Leh was very clearly visible, with the Khardong range of hills, still under snow, behind us. We were then shown the temple room, which, after Hemis, was surprisingly clean. It contained the usual row of idols, manifestations of Buddha, before which lights were burning, and several good Lhasa scrolls. Meanwile the Rani had been arraying herself in her best clothes in response to my request for permission to photograph the family. The younger boy disappeared in an excess of shyness, but I obtained a photograph of the Raja, Rani and their elder son, and R.T. took another with me included in the group.

R.T. and I then retired to eat the lunch we had brought with us; the Raja had kindly provided food for us but we thought it wiser to act on Jeeves' suggestion and let him take it away for our Mohammedan servants; it had been prepared by Mohammedans, so our men had no objection to eating it, and pronounced it excellent.

After lunch the Raja and his family returned and presented me with an ornamental wooden box painted in orange and gold, and a sandy-coloured jade cup standing on an embossed white metal (local silver?) base and with a lid of the same white metal topped with a red stone; both base and lid were painted in places with gold. My presents in return consisted of some saffron (this apparently is used in Lamaistic ritual and highly prized) and the pair to the chromium holder I had given to the Hemis monastery.

The Drivers dined with us on the 22nd, the wireless set letting us down by barely functioning at all. Hitler has apparently demanded that French plenipotentiaries be appointed to hear and answer his terms. I imagine the terms will be light, in order that the French may have no difficulty in accepting them; once France is disarmed and unable to resist, Hitler can impose what terms he will, irrespective of any pledge he may for his part have given France. The fate of the French fleet and, to a lesser extent, that of their Air Force, will be a large factor in the future course of the war; but I cannot imagine any Captain of a French vessel, able to steam out to sea and join the British naval forces, tamely surrendering his ship whatever his Government may say.

We attended the morning service at the Moravian Mission Church on Sunday the 23rd. The service was taken by an elderly Ladakhi pastor and was of course in Buddhi; two of the hymns could be sung in English, however, so I was able to join in them. The congregation, excluding Mr. and Mrs. Driver (the former of whom played the harmonium), Ann Driver, R.T. and me, numbered 28, the sexes being fairly equally represented but divided one from the other by the aisle; the Europeans sat on a bench, the rest on rugs.

After breakfast on the 24th we climbed up to the old castle of the Kings of Ladakh that overlooks the town from the east. The castle is seven stories high and solidly built; no one, including the present Raja, has been able to tell me its age, but four or five hundred years seems to be the general estimate and I should say the former is more nearly right than the latter. The Raja was of course in Stok, and we were therefore shown round by some of the Lamas who live in the Castle and look after the private temples and rooms set aside for religious purposes, which are, or seem to be, the only parts of the Castle now furnished and inhabited, though the building is in no way in disrepair. In pleasant contrast to Hemis, the temple rooms were clean and airy, but remarkable in no other respect, housing rows of idols draped in coloured cloth. The only idol of any note was a gigantic one of a Buddha towering up through the ceiling of the first floor into the second storey.

This afternoon I received a code telegram from Peter Hailey regarding the possibility of accommodating extra troops in the Serai. I wired back saying that accommodation is available, but followed up the telegram with a letter in which I have asked that the whole subject of military arrangements in Ladakh should be reviewed by a competent officer and given my own rather hurried views in the matter. I'm afraid nothing will come of it, though the question badly needs consideration; it is probably not one of my duties as B.J.C. to throw pebbles into the Kashmir Government's calm pool in which they have drowned their military responsibilities for this part of India's frontier, but I shall be happier if even an unauthorised pebble causes a slight ripple.

We visited the Sankar Monastery, a mile to the north of Leh, on the 25th morning, and were very pleased to find it scrupulously clean and well-kept. The Lamas, who were cheerful and friendly and who seem rightly to take their obligations seriously, showed us round with obvious pride in their monastery, and explained that as their Skushog (the final "g" is pronounced as a "k") is in Lhasa they are taking extra pains to keep the place in good order. I was presented on leaving with a sand-coloured jade cup (a nice clear one) in its Tibetan stand—the Khan Sahib had well-meaningly but (to me) rather embarrassingly primed the Lamas that I like jade—and I in return asked what the Monastery would like, the Khan Sahib having already told me that they were anxious to obtain wood. The Manager of the Monastery promptly asked for a couple of trees, a request I had no difficulty in granting as one part of the Residency garden is greatly over-wooded. All I could give however was permission to cut the trees, because as the Residency is rented from the Kashmir Government the trees, when cut, are their property. The Khan Sahib undertook to arrange matters, and has since obtained the trees free for the monastery.

I left Leh at 8.30 a.m. on the 29th on tour to the Shyok valley; R.T. remained behind. I have in fact brought only Jafar Ali (the Jemadar Chuprassi), Habiba (second Chuprassi), Ghulam Ali (Sub-Overseer of this section of the Road and, it happens, Jafar's brother) and Jeeves, who will have to cook my meals in addition to his other duties.

During the first day's march I halted at Trigtse Lamasery at the invitation of one of its Lamas who met me by the way. The Lamasery is an imposing edifice, its buildings covering one side of a hill surmounted by the main temple, but fell far short of Sankar Goupa's standard of cleanliness, and its idols and religious paraphernalia were not remarkable. I presented the Lamas with an ornate cup, eight inches high, smothered in an enamelled floral design, and was given a painted scroll surrounded by an embroidered prayer in Thibetan. The painting is delicate and artistic, and, I believe, old Chinese—at all events Chinese characters appear in between the verses of the prayer. I must find out what I can about this "tánka" from the Drivers; I felt rather ashamed of my tawdry modern present, which suffered in comparison with the scroll I had been given, but the Lamas seemed very pleased with it.

We halted for the night at Ranbirpore, 14 miles from Leh. The march was a very easy one and took us only 5 hours, including the visit to the Monastery. Ranbirpore, due east of Leh, was, I understand, once a cantonment and a large town; it is now mainly derelict and tumbledown, and the people seem more than ordinarily poor.

Our second march, on the 30th, was also an easy one, to Sakti, and also of 14 miles, gradually ascending. I left Ranbirpore at 8 a.m. and rode all but the first mile or mile and a half, reaching Sakti at 11.45.

The march to Tsultak on the 1st July seemed to me the most difficult, so far, of the whole tour, though only one of 16 miles. Shortly after leaving Sakti the path began to ascend and continued to do so, zigzagging up the stony hillside, for what seemed an interminable distance. Long before the summit of the Chang La was reached we found that the track had been obliterated by innumerable rivulets caused by melted snow, and the ponies had great difficulty in negotiating the Pass. I later learned that two of the baggage-ponies had found themselves unequal to it, when loaded. Though there was little snow at the top of the Pass our troubles were not over when we reached the summit, for there was a bitterly cold wind blowing and the road on the far side was no better than that on the ascent. I reached Tsultak at 1.45, having begun the march at 8; the baggage-train did not arrive until 5.15 a.m. The only pleasant thing about the march was the number of Alpine flowers met with towards the top of the Chang La. Once more I wished I had with me a book about Kashmir's flora. There were tiny forget-me-nots, and another tiny dark blue flower, and yellow flowers like miniature buttercups, and dark purple, so dark as to be almost black, flowers something like wild hyacinths, but smaller and with spiked pistils, and purple wild primulas.

Our camp-site was on the edge of a small lake. The water would have invited me to bathe had it not been so icy cold. A family of duck, father, mother and four babies just learning to swim, inhabit the lake. I could not get close enough to distinguish them with certainty, but I think they are Ruddy Sheldrake.

After a very cold night we left Tsultak at 8 a.m. intending to march to Shyok. A woman met us on arrival in the Durgab Nullah, however, with the news that a bridge had been washed away farther down the stream and that we should have to wait for it to be repaired before we could go on to Shyok. The Sub-Overseer went ahead while I waited for an hour by the river. As it seemed improbable that the bridge, wherever it was, could be so well repaired as to take the baggage-ponies I ordered the tents to be pitched where I was, and rode on towards Shyok. Some four miles short of the village I found that not one one but two bridges had been completely washed away, and that the river was fordable by pony at the site of the first bridge it was decidedly not at that of the second. Since to rebuilt the second bridge was obviously a matter of days and not hours I had to give up the idea of reaching Shyok, which for this year will have to go uninspected; there is in any case only a Serai there. I climbed up a precipitous hill (on, of course, the wrong side of the river) from which I could see the road to the village; it seems in good order, as, indeed, one would expect it to be, as the man responsible knew I should inspect it. I see no reason for having the two bridges where they were; they cross a turbulent stream, whereas one bridge across a more placid tributary higher up will do the job just as well and stand far less chance of being washed away. I have therefore "issued orders accordingly", and the ass of an Overseer must bear the cost—partly because he might have thought of all this last year, before building two useless bridges, and partly because he must (or should) have known that the bridges had gone long before I got this far. There seems to have been a passion for building bridges on new alignments of the road; to shorten the distance between A and B is an excellent thing provided the new alignment and its bridges are going to stand the flood-season, but what I have seen so far has not done so, with the result that the new road is utterly unusable. Fewer bridges and a better road (the travellers who followed the old alignment were not altogether fools) seems a sounder maxim, and certainly a cheaper one. In 400 odd miles an extra mile or so won't make much difference, and the ideal should, I feel, be a reasonably well-surfaced road passable in all weather—an unattainable ideal, I would add, for passes and mountain-streams defy road-making with a grant of Rs.2000 p.a. to do it on.

We completed the 28 miles' journey to Leh on the 4th July. I left Sakti at 7 a.m., reached Ranbirpore, 14 miles away, at 10.30, and Leh at 1.45 p.m. The baggage got in at about 6 p.m., the ponies and coolies seeming none the worse for their long journey—the longest day's march we have done so far.

The battery of the wireless set has now failed completely and we have to rely on week-old papers for our news. The war seems very far away.

I left Leh for my tour to the Nubra at 7 a.m. on the 10th, having sent my kit off in advance, as I intend to double the first two marches. We reached Pulo, ordinarily one's first stage, at 9.30 a.m., after a steady but not difficult 10 miles' ascent. Pulo is 15,000 ft. above sea level, and is at the foot of the last steep ascent up the Khardong Pass. A yak was provided for me but I found its ridged back, even covered with a double layer of coarse local blanket, very far from comfortable, and I dismounted after 10 minutes' fidgetting. We were at the crest of the Pass at 11.30. There was a good deal of snow on the far side, but lower down we came to patches of turf and large clumps of wild primulas. I saw several brown marmots, as I had done on the Chang La. We halted at 12 noon for three-quarters of an hour, and then began the long descent into the valley. Fortunately the road was in very good order and we arrived in Khardong village at 3.30 p.m., a very satisfactory timing for a 27 mile march which included a 17,600ft. Pass. Khardong village itself is 13,500 feet above sea level.

We struck camp at 8 a.m. this morning, the 11th July. I was to discover that this late start was a mistake, for although the distance to Thirit, our halting place, was only 16 miles according to the Polymetrical Tables from which my route was taken, it included two very steep and long ascents, and the present-day road is, I think, considerably longer than that which was followed when the Tables were compiled. As a result I reached Thirit at 1.45, after a half-hour's halt at Khalsar, but the baggage-train did not arrive until 5 p.m.

From Khardong Village the road descends sharply into a narrow gorge and for five or six miles runs through a delightful grove of tamarisk trees and willows, sprinkled with wild rose bushes. I was sorry when the gorge debouched into the wide Shyok nullah, sandy and hot. We were not to continue in the nullah for long, however, but soon began a long ascent up the hillside. Sati, a village at which there is a serai for the maintenance of which the B.J.C. is responsible, is on the other side of the nullah; there is no bridge and the Shyok, at all events for some miles on either side of Sati, is unfordable, so I was unable to inspect the serai. I have arranged to have a boat of some sort ready on my return journey, and propose to make my way along the hills on the Sati side of the river to the village, see the serai, cross the Shyok in the boat, and join the horses at the junction of the Shyok and Khardong nullahs. The serai, in view of the altered position of the road, seems to me to have lost its use, but I suppose I had better see it.

From the high ground to which we had laboriously climbed, the waters of the Shyok and the Khardong gorge stream were an interesting contrast to each other: the former were muddy, the latter clear and sea-green but ending abruptly in an almost straight line where they entered the Shyok.

The road descended from the high ground into the village of Khalsar, tucked into a narrow valley at right angles to the Shyok nullah. I halted in a small spinney for half an hour or so and had lunch: milk chocolate, biscuits and coffee, the only kind of lunch I feel capable of facing during a march.

Once the far side of the Khalsar nullah had been climbed our road ran across a stony, uneven plateau, from the northern edge of which we had a pleasing view of the junction of the Nubra and Shyok valleys, with Thirit lying at the mouth of the former. From this plateau we dropped into the Shyok valley and crossed it to the new bridge near Sati; the bridge looks imposing, and is maintained by the Kashmir Government. I have an idea that however well they may look, most of the bridges on the Treaty Road would, at the first sign of bad weather or flood, meet the fate of those constructed by "Potiphar Gubbins, C.E.":

"Every bridge that he makes either buckles or breaks . . .", and I would put no money on the Sati bridge surviving another serious flood of the Shyok.

The new battery for the wireless set arrived on the 9th, the day before I left on this tour, so I was able to hear the evening news bulletins. At present I am in the world but not of it—so far away that events in Europe seem unreal and almost insignificant, a position conducive to that "wishful thinking" that we are warned so much against nowadays; the slightest expression of optimism seems to be condemned as "wishful thinking", though any opinion to the contrary is equally condemned, as unpatriotic "defeatism"—another catchword. Apparently the only safe attitude to adopt is to have no opinion about anything.

The first 10 or 11 miles of our march this morning, the 13th July, continued along the Nubra valley, to the east and against the flow of the river. The path was very stony and vegetation became progressively less and less. At Turmpalli the track turned right-handed towards the hills and for the next hour we zigzagged up the face of the mountains, as steep and difficult an ascent as any we have yet encountered. From the crest we dropped down into a narrow gorge at the bottom of which tumbled a muddy snow-water stream. Umlung, the halting-place suggested by the Polymetrical Tables, proved to be a flat, stony stretch of ground about 20 yards square, devoid of vegetation but littered with the bones of two or three ponies. Tashi Nurbu, the overseer of this section of the road, told me that we should come to another and more suitable camp-site in another two miles, so I decided to go on. The two miles took us over an hour to cover, and ended in a breathless scramble up an almost perpendicular hillside. We had left Panamik at 7 a.m., halting for 20 minutes en route, and reached our halting-place at 1 p.m., the distance travelled being about 17 miles; the kit arrived at 4 p.m. The "more suitable camp-site", though better than Umlung, is a small plateau between barren hills, stony, bleak and sandy, with a few clumps of coarse grass and yellowish-green flowers like small Canterbury Bells. It is the worst camping-ground we have used, and instead of spending two days here, as I had intended, I have decided to send the kit back to Panamik to-morrow and to push on early to Tutyalak and then get back to Panamik for the night. This

1. (right) *Kate Georgina Fry, nee Stewart, grandmother of Leslie Fry*

2. (below) *Extract from diary of Kate Georgina Fry, kept when she moved with the 1st Battalion Rifle Brigade, as Headmistress of the Battalion School, to India in 1881*

3 and 4. Tiger shot by Leslie Fry

5. Sir Leslie Fry

6. 'The Household Cavalry'; Sultan, Faiz, and Jeeves

7. *Crossing the snow*

8. *View from the top of Zoji La*

will mean a very long march for Tashi Nurbu, Ghulam Rasul (my syce) and me, but anything, I feel, would be better than another day here; as the ponies and coolies must have a rest we shall halt at Panamik the day after to-morrow. There is little point in going further; the track such as it is, continues to the Karakoram in much the same dilapidated condition it is in from the Shyok to this unnamed and desolate spot, and my looking at it won't improve it. To put this section of the road into a state of repair comparable with that of the Srinagar-Leh section would take a very considerable sum of money, the best part of a year's grant for the whole road, and such expenditure would, I think, be unjustified until there is a likelihood of trade reviving.

Leaving the baggage-train, under Jafar Ali, to make its way back to Panamik, Tashi Nurbu, Ghulam and I this morning, the 14th July, went forward towards Tutyalak. The track was narrow, stony and very undulating, and I found walking easier than riding. We had not gone very far when we met Harji Lal returning from his tour. Harji Lal, whom I had not met before, was formerly Haib Tehsildar of Leh, but acquired (probably rightly) a reputation for dishonesty and extorting bribes, and was transferred from Leh last year after falling foul of Peter Hailey—whether Peter was instrumental in securing the transfer I do not know. Ten days or so ago Harji Lal re-appeared in Leh as Special Officer appointed by the Kashmir Government to watch the movements of foreigners in the District and generally to act as an Intelligence agent, a most unsuitable choice for such a post. I understand he has recently arrested two Yarkandis travelling to Leh; if, as seems likely, he arrested them on the Treaty Road his action was altogether *ultra vires*, for only the Joint Commissioners have jurisdiction on the Road, and any usurpation of their jurisdiction cannot be tolerated. I shall look into the matter when I get back to Leh, and devoutly hope that the position turns out to be as I suspect, for I shall then have an excellent opportunity for representing the whole business to the Residency in an attempt to get Mr. Harji Lal out of Ladakh again.

We went as far as Tutyalak Bridge, or the site of it, for the bridge was washed away two or three years ago and has not been re-made. The position since then has been that the original road on the one side of the nullah, although straight and almost flat, has been disused for want of a bridge at the end of it, while a new road, on the other side (the Tutyalak side) of the nullah has been made. The new track is, as I have said, very difficult, but the bridge at the beginning of it—for the stream obviously had in any case to be bridged somewhere—looks impregnable. The upkeep of the new track will probably cost as much as annual repairs to the old bridge would, and cause more inconvenience to travellers, but I do not intend to make any change of policy. The new track will, however, need a good deal of improvement.

Our return journey was considerably easier than the march from Panamik to Umlung had been, and we were back again in the Nubra valley at 11.30. We halted for an hour at 1 p.m. and reached our camp in Panamik at 3.20 p.m., to find the tents already pitched and the tea ready.

We remained in Panamik on the 15th and enjoyed a completely idle day. Harji Lal paid me a visit in the morning and told me, among other things, that he had not arrested the two Yarkandis but merely sent them back to Leh under police escort because, he said, he realised he had no jurisdiction on the Road. I replied that I could see no difference between a formal arrest of the men and their being placed in police custody; if there were a distinction it was that the former had a legal colour, *ultra vires* though it would be, but the latter was both *ultra vires* and altogether illegal because no charge had been preferred. I said I would consult my Joint Commissioner on my return to Leh; it is clearly necessary to do this before making any other move because Harji Lal derives his authority direct from the Kashmir Government and any successful action on my part can therefore only be taken with the support of the State Joint Commissioner—or, rather, his support would be of very great help.

I completed the short march from Panamik to Tegur in 3½ hours on the 16th, and in the afternoon visited the local monastery, newly rebuilt. It has a lovely view over the Nubra valley but is otherwise without interest.

Leaving Tegur at 8 a.m. on the 17th I reached Thirit just before 10 and the Sati Bridge (though it is, in fact, at least four miles from Sati) at 11 a.m. I sent Ghulam Rasul with the ponies across the bridge and on to Khalsar, and continued along the east bank of the river myself, accompanied by Tashi Nurbu. A boat had been duly prepared for the crossing of the Shyok river to Khalsar. It consisted of about a dozen goat and sheep skins blown up tight and tied Heath-Robinson fashion to a number of bamboo poles.

From Khalsar, I completed the short march to Khardong Village in 3½ hours on the 18th July. Next day we left at 7 a.m. and were at the top of the pass shortly after 11. There was far less snow about than there had been on our outward journey, but patches of ice made the going difficult in places, and it was impossible to ride up the final ascent. We halted for lunch at Pulo at about 12.15, and after nearly an hour's rest, began the final 10 miles to Leh, arriving at 3.30 p.m. The view from the top of the Pass was magnificent, though visibility was not good. Mt. Godwin Austen is said to be visible to the north of the Khardong, but I was unable to distinguish it. To the South Leh seemed very green at the end of the brown valley running down the Pass, and beyond it Stog was very clear; the horizon was bounded by a ridge of snow-clad peaks in a long line against the sky. Our journey was over.'

Chapter Five

INDIA: INDEPENDENCE, 1947/1948

In his administrative capacity as Deputy Secretary to the External Affairs Department of India from 1946 until the transfer of power in 1947, 'Bunny' Fry witnessed the unheaval of the days that led to independence in close-up. His Minister for that period was to go down in history as one of the architects of the new structure: Pandit Jawarharlal Nehru. Through Leslie's work they became known to each other personally, and occasionally Leslie would accompany the Minister to meetings of the Indian Cabinet. His experience of India—as soldier and administrator—was so extensive and solidly founded that Nehru suggested that he should remain with the new Government of India. It must have been a tempting offer; and one that would have appealed to many members of 'the Raj' who were watching their careers take a turn for the unknown. But Leslie Fry thought it better not to accept. It is true that he was very much in tune with Macaulay's prophecy, that India 'might in some future age demand European institutions', and believed with him that such a day—however problematic to the administration caught momentarily between the two régimes—would be 'the proudest day in English history'. This did not, however, imply to Leslie's way of thinking that the English had to outstay the event.

In his view, in any case, it seemed impossible for the British to stay where they were. Even had the concept of an orderly, phased withdrawal from power been accepted, which was most improbable to Leslie's ideas, events would quickly have overtaken the programme. And it would not have needed violence to rid India of its British community at that stage. The passive resistance advocated by Mahatma Gandhi would have done the trick had it been applied with any assiduity. A general strike, embargo on food supplies, embargo on work for the British in any form—these would, Leslie believed, have led to immediate capitulation. He deemed it wiser to accept realities, fix an early date for the transfer of power, and get out.

In his analysis of the pros and cons of a hasty withdrawal, which is what the transfer seemed when it came to it, Leslie found that the leaders of the Indian National Congress Party, notably Mahatma Gandhi, Pandit Nehru and Sardar Patel (the 'iron man of India'), were most unlikely to accept delay. Moreover, the pressure of the Muslim League, led by

Mohammed Ali Jinnah and Liaquat Ali Khan, for the creation of a separate Muslim State (Pakistan) made the situation potentially chaotic and bloody if the timing were not hastened. It is not surprising that the idea of a phased, perhaps five-year withdrawal, came largely from those who were not in India by the end of the war, and were engrossed with mammoth problems elsewhere.

This aftermath of war had, however, not left India unmarked. For the British members of the Indian Services, 1946, and the first months of 1947, had been an extremely anxious time. The tense political situation, the uncertain future for British residents, made it difficult to concentrate on the other tasks in hand. Leslie himself enjoyed Crown service, and wanted to stay in it, even if it meant leaving India, where so few of his colleagues could hope to be absorbed into the new scene. His choice of the temporary post in the High Commission for the United Kingdom recently set up in New Delhi meant that for the remaining, historic time he was at least at the hub of things.

The pen which he put down as Deputy Secretary to the External Affairs Department was metaphorically picked up again half an hour later, on the 23rd June 1947, in the office of the High Commission. The building was on the other side of the road from the grounds of the house in which Mahatma Gandhi was shortly afterwards assassinated. The shot was clearly audible from where Leslie Fry was sitting at his desk.

*   *   *   *   *

'As luck would have it', perhaps the first of a long series of incredible coincidences by which he always seemed to catch the big moments in history, Leslie was also in Delhi on the day which began at midnight on 14th August 1947, with the transference of power from British to Indian hands, and continued into 24 hours of ceremonial, confusion, and celebration in which literally hundreds of thousands of people surged to take part.

Leslie himself had a pass to allow him into the Legislative Assembly Chamber for the ceremonial there. But to reach the Assembly he had to make his way through a daunting sequence of formal and informal parades. The Delhi parade ground was by the early hours so crammed with people that the main procession had to be cancelled. Leslie failed even to reach the saluting base where the tricolour of India was to be flown for the first time. The flag was eventually raised not from below the flagstaff, but from Lord Mountbatten's ceremonial coach . . . by Pandit Nehru himself.

*   *   *   *   *

There is no doubt that the further two years working in India (as a founder-member of the United Kingdom High Commission in New Delhi) which were now granted to Leslie Fry provided him with a stimulating view of the process of Independence and its aftermath. It was as the only British official observer, in fact, that he became involved in the confused and controversial run-up to India's resolve to annexe the State of Hyderabad. As in many other regions of the whole sub-continent, violence and possibly extremely bloody civil riots were still threatening, and it seemed advisable to undertake the evacuation of British and other nationals before the confrontation came to a head. His previous service in Hyderabad and his military experience made Leslie an obvious choice for this undertaking, and his personal reports and despatches on the overall situation showed that he had a total grasp of what was at stake. In later years he admitted that he took a step against all his instincts as a professional soldier, and actually volunteered! But with the 30th anniversary of the evacuation of Hyderabad imminent as we go to press with Leslie Fry's memoirs, it is not to be regretted that he did. The account he has left of the whole event is both a considered, knowledgeable document and a very human story.

*   *   *   *   *

Hyderabad City, together with its suburbs of Secunderabad, Trimulgherry and Bolarum, is the fourth largest urban area of the Indian sub-continent. the city housed the Muslim hierarchy of the State, the State Forces, Police and Government officials; its population was predominantly Muslim. It was in the suburbs that the British and Indian Army units had been stationed, forming one of the biggest garrisons in the Empire; and the district was therefore under British administration. As Under-Secretary to the Resident in Hyderabad in 1935 Leslie Fry had held the appointment of District Magistrate in the British-administered areas of the State, and perforce spent a good deal of his time hearing court cases.

A very senior officer of the Political Service once described Hyderabad State as 'redolent of intrigue'. At the centre of the web had always been His Exalted Highness the Nizam, careful in the tradition of his dynasty to allow no Prime Minister of his to become too powerful. Shrewd, yet wholly out of touch with events; obstinate, swayed by prejudice and preferring to hear advice of his liking; feudal in outlook, but sincere in his wish to be the father of his people, he had always been prominently characterised by cupidity. It was, Leslie Fry believed, that attribute in the main which caused him initially to follow the will-o'-the-wisp of independence, listening only to those who counselled a policy which might bring him profit or at least permit him to retain that which he had of power and wealth.

It was represented to him, moreover, that his whole position and perhaps his life itself depended on the support of the loyal Ittehad-ul-Muslimeen (with Pakistan behind it).

In November 1947 a Standstill Agreement was signed which was to govern Indo-Hyderabad relations for one year. This, however, was born in an atmosphere of suspicion and ill-will, owing largely to the Ittehad-ul-Muslimeen's success in ousting the Nawab of Chhatari, Sir Sultan Ahmed and Sir Walter Monckton from the Nizam's counsels and replacing them by a régime representing extremist Muslim elements. Mir Laik Ali twice declined the appointment of Prime Minister of the State when the Nawab of Chhatari demitted office, and was finally ordered by the Nizam to accept it.

Lord Mountbatten did his best to persuade the Nizam that Hyderabad's future could lie only in close association with India. He failed, and when he left India the only question—provided Hyderabad did not capitulate—was the actual timing of India's direct action against the State. On the 7th September, after months of rising tension, the Indian Government issued what was a virtual ultimatum requiring the Nizam to facilitate the return of Indian Army units to the old British Indian Army barracks in Secunderabad and the neighbouring cantonments. On Hyderabad rejecting this, the Indian Government declared themselves free to take whatever action they might consider necessary.

It is generally believed that 4 a.m. on the night of the 12th/13th September was the time set for the opening of India's action, though it is clear that at one point Indian Union troops were by then at least 20 miles within the State frontier.

Lieut.-General Rajendrasinhji was in supreme command of the operation, with his headquarters at Poona. He had served with the 2nd Royal Lancers and won a very good D.S.C. in the Western Desert campaign of the Second World War. Major-General Chaudhri commanded the first units to reach Secunderabad.

The State Forces mobilised to meet the invading units of the Indian Army consisted of:

Four regiments of cavalry, maintained for ceremonial purposes but used in this affair as infantry;

ten 25-pounder guns (of which two were immediately lost, as they had been placed on the far side of a bridge which was then demolished);

eleven battalions of infantry of which three were under strength and another two and a half composed of Muslim refugees who had been so short a time under arms that they had not fired a musketry course;

the Razakars (the Home Guard as they were intended to be) which had been raised by Kazim Razvi were completely useless: they turned tail at the first shot.

The Hyderabad regular army fought well enough, but the overwhelmingly powerful Indian army units, veterans of the Second World War, superbly led and armed, swept all before them and could have reached Secunderabad, their objective, in two days instead of the four they actually took.

With the State capital threatened on three sides, his men straggling back in defeat and the garrison in the city preparing for a last stand, General El Edroos explained to the Hyderabad Government that further resistance could result only in wanton waste of life. The Government, however, were in favour of continuing the struggle and the General therefore placed his advice before the Nizam personally on the morning of the 17th September. It was accepted; the Government tendered their resignations; the unconditional surrender of Hyderabad State was announced from Deccan radio station, in Hyderabad City; and hostilities ended at 5 p.m. that afternoon.

Kazim Razvi was at once arrested by Hyderabad troops themselves and handed over to the Indian Military Governor, Major-General Chaudhri, who had established his headquarters in the old Residency building at Bolarum. The Nizam made two speeches from Deccan radio, the first announcing the surrender of the State and placing responsibility for recent events firmly on the Mir Laik Ali Ministry 'who ought to have resigned long ago'. Yet it was the Nizam, it will be recalled, who had insisted on Mir Laik Ali's accepting the Premiership. The second speech, Leslie Fry had on good authority, was drafted by Munshi himself.

To return to the events that led eventually to the organised evacuation of British and other nationals from the scene of this débâcle: the situation began to look potentially dangerous with the Standstill Agreement of November 1947, and the ink was hardly dry on it before the Indian National Congress Party in the State began a campaign for responsible government in Hyderabad, with threats of civil disobedience if this demand was not conceded.

The Indian Government, for their part, introduced restrictions on the movement into the State of a wide range of goods, such as petrol, lubricants, chemicals, and machinery. The reason given for this was that such materials would increase Hyderabad State's military potential.

Further heavy pressure was brought to bear on the State by the infiltration into it (notably from the Bezwada District of Madras) of armed groups of Communists.

In its issue dated the 4th October 1948 *The Times of India* reported on an informal talk with journalists in Secunderabad the day before, the 3rd October, by the Publicity Secretary of the Hyderabad State Congress Party. He claimed that, operating from outside the State, camps were established all along the border and smashed 500 of the 750 State Customs outposts on the frontier. Shortly afterwards State Congress workers entered the State at 82 different points and dislocated all telephone, telegraph and rail communications. As a result, Hyderabad State was cut off entirely from the rest of India.

On some date, probably late in August or early in September 1948, the State Government addressed a letter to the President of the Security Council of the United Nations complaining that India's pressure on the State constituted a threat to peace. India declared this appeal invalid, holding that the dispute was domestic and that under the Standstill Agreement of November 1947 Hyderabad had no international *locus standi.*

The reference to the United Nations was later countermanded by the Nizam.

By then, having made a first reconnaissance in the July—and been totally ignored by the Hyderabad Government—Leslie Fry had begun the organisation of the evacuation. The story is one that exists, fortunately, in his own words:

'British officials have evacuated British subjects, and sometimes friendly nationals also, on scores of occasions and no doubt will have to carry out such operations many times again. The problem, *mutatis mutandis,* are almost always the same. Timing: too early a move may cause panic, yet to delay a move too long may render it either impossible or disorderly; how many people will in the event wish to leave, how are they to be brought together at the point of embarkation, whether by sea or by air; how are they to be warned to be ready to leave their homes; and how are they to be fed and otherwise maintained if there is a gap between their leaving their homes and the embarkation?

Above all, there is the problem of the advice which they are to be given. Obviously no-one can be ordered to leave. The official in charge, whether an Ambassador to the country which unhappily is in turmoil, or a single individual such as I in Hyderabad State, can do no more than ascertain the whereabouts of those for whose protection he is responsible, arrange means by which he can keep in constant touch with them, explain the evacuation procedure which will be adopted should a move be thought desirable, and then leave it to his flock to decide for themselves whether to take advantage of the arrangements which are being put in hand.

In a number of instances, people will ask his advice: what do you think we should do, go or stay? There is no firm answer that can be given to such a question. Not only do family circumstances differ: elderly people, for instance, living outside danger areas, might well prefer to stay where they were; younger couples, with children, would probably choose to move. But in every case the people concerned must be made to see that the choice is for them alone to make.

In Hyderabad, several Missionary Societies were operating, Anglican, Episcopalian (U.S. and Canadian), and Roman Catholic. I got in touch

with the leaders of all of them as soon as possible after my arrival in
the State, explained my mission, took lists of their staff and arranged ways
and means of keeping in touch. None showed any wish to move: their
clear duty was to remain with their people.

Others who had no intention of moving were the British officials working with the Hyderabad State Railway and similar Departments.

The official responsible for any evacuation would be well advised to
make his mind up from the start to suffer criticism of one kind or another.
If in the event the general hurly-burly proves to be less dangerous than
had been feared, then why had people been more or less encouraged
to leave? Or if conditions deteriorate so badly that lives and property are
seriously at risk, then why had he not positively insisted on people getting
out while they could still do so?'

*　　*　　*　　*　　*

'About 500 British Subjects were living in Hyderabad State, as were a
number of Canadians and Americans, in both cases mainly Protestant
missionaries. There was also a sprinkling of citizens of other countries.

If it came to hostilities, of themselves they would represent little danger
to foreigners in the State; should any suffer injury it would be by sheer
bad luck. Neither side would be shooting deliberately at them, the Indian
Air Force would certainly not bomb civilian residential areas and any
serious fighting which took place would surely be in open country.

It was inconceivable moreover that hostilities could last more
than three or four days. However gallant, seven Battalions of Hyderabad
Infantry would be no match for an Army in their way as professional
and experienced in battle as any in the world. An Indian Armoured
Division had only to sweep into the State from one or more of numerous
possible points of entry, brush aside the ground forces opposing it and
capture the Nizam and his Government in their own capital.

Foreigners might nevertheless find themselves in very real danger if
communal rioting began. As soon as news of an Indian invasion broke,
the more hot-heated of the Hindu majority might rise against their Muslim
masters and foreigners then find themselves caught in the ensuing carnage
and arson. A murderous mob is no respecter of persons and property.
The Punjab, many other areas and even Delhi itself in the autumn of
1947 bore witness to that.

Uninterrupted communications with the High Commission was going
therefore to be important. If hostilities broke out, telegraph and telephone
services, would at best become heavily overloaded and might well be
suspended altogether. Wireless would solve that problem, but I wished
to have no trouble with the Indian authorities about a licence for the
possession of a transmitting set.

I accordingly went to the External Affairs Department and explained to a senior official, a friend of mine, what I was proposing to do and why I was seeking agreement to my taking wireless transmitting apparatus into Hyderabad State with me.

He said that he did not suppose the Government of India would agree to my possessing such apparatus, particularly in Hyderabad. Clearly they could not prevent my going there, but all sorts of objections and complications might arise if it became known that I was able to send information out through channels other than those provided by public services.

I replied that as things stood the constitutional status of Hyderabad was undefined, but whatever it was the State was certainly not Indian territory. I should be the representative there of the United Kingdom High Commission and so, by extension, of the British Government. It was a well-established principle that diplomatic representatives and their Governments had the right to communicate with each other by all available means and at all times. Such niceties aside, however, it would be utterly impossible for me to evacuate British Subjects in an emergency unless the High Commission and I were able to contact each other direct, without delay, at any hour of the day or night.

The official asked me to wait while he consulted a colleague. When he came back he said that he was sorry, but his answer was the same.

I told him that I should be ashamed to report to the High Commission that the Government of India, which I had served for many years, was unwilling to facilitate the protection of British Subjects in an emergency. This attitude would cause not only astonishment but resentment in Britain. I hoped therefore that he would see no objection if I continued to wait in the Department while he consulted other colleagues of his, who might take a more favourable view of my request. I was prepared to wait indefinitely, for I had been long enough in India to learn, if nothing else, that time really was of no consequence. This was said with a smile. Almost anything can be said, with a smile.

He took my obstinacy in good part and, though he held out no hope of a change of mind, went off for more consultations. They took rather a long time. Eventually he came back and said that I might take the apparatus with me into Hyderabad provided I promised to use it only for messages concerned with the welfare of British Subjects or other foreign nationals. It was not to be used for any message of a political or military nature. I accepted that restriction, and the agreement at which we had arrived was confirmed in writing as soon as I got back to the High Commission. That was three hours after my request had first been made.

Certain friendly Missions, such as the Canadian High Commission and the U.S. Embassy, known to have nationals in Hyderabad were told that I was going to the State. They provided me with lists of their people's names and addresses, and asked me to do anything possible to help should they find themselves in difficulty.

Shortly afterwards, with the appropriate receiving and transmitting apparatus among our luggage, a wireless operator from the High Commission and I entered Hyderabad State. Hughes had been parachuted into Yugoslavia in the War to serve with Tito's partisans and was admirably equipped to take on our present job. I installed him in a suite of rooms on the top floor of a boarding-house run by an elderly Anglo-Indian woman, where his apparatus would be relatively unobtrusive, and took a room for myself in the Secunderabad Club not more than half-a-mile away. To save his having to conceal his wireless equipment and cypher books in a hurry if he heard someone coming up the stairs to his suite, I used to herald my arrival by whistling "The British Grenadiers". A little cloak-and-dagger stuff is always stimulating.

The next step, not merely as a matter of courtesy but to secure at least its benevolent acquiescence in my activities, was to make something of my purpose known to the Nizam's Government. I therefore arranged to call on the Chief Secretary.

He plainly was disappointed to find that I had brought no message from London with me, but assured me that the State authorities would give me any reasonable assistance they could.

In the course of checking and amending the lists of the British, Canadian, American and other nationals in the State with which I had been provided in Delhi it quickly became apparent that by no means all of them would wish to be evacuated in the event of hostilities or serious communal rioting. Clearly there could be no question of ordering people to go; one could only offer advice.

Nevertheless, there remained the responsibility, as I saw it, of trying to ensure that the risk to those who stayed behind was reduced to a minimum. When therefore I was able to form a reasonably accurate estimate of those who wished to be evacuated and those who would choose to stay, I made a discreet search for a suitable set of buildings in which if necessary to concentrate the stayers. Concentration obviously would simplify supply and transport problems should food and petrol become scarce, as indeed happened, or need arise for a second evacuation. Moreover, in times of grave uncertainty or danger the physical proximity of one's own kind, a sense of togetherness, can be a comfort to many people.

An ideal place came to light almost at once. This was a factory which had been set up in the War for the production of Bren guns. That it had made only a prototype by the end of 1945 is neither here nor there. It might have been designed for exactly my purpose.

It took the form of a square fort with thick stone walls about twelve feet high. At each corner stood a turret with loopholes in it through which excellent visibility could be had over a considerable distance; and it possessed only one entrance, through a pair of massive gates which could be bolted and barred. It would have fitted admirably into a film about the Foreign Legion. But why, it may be asked, should a Bren gun factory be so designed? The only reason I can offer is that the factory buildings and their lethal products had to be protected from sabotage and theft.

At a short distance from the main gate were two rows of comfortable bungalows which had been put up for the officials and senior workmen of the factory. A few were occupied by the employees of a British Company making cement in some of the factory buildings, but the majority were empty. All were provided with water and electricity.

The factory was about five miles from the twin cities of Hyderabad, the capital, and Secunderabad, the cantonment area which before 1947 had held one of the biggest British garrisons in Asia. This made the place even more attractive. It was well removed from the densely populated quarters in which communal rioting was most likely to break out and its precise position could be reported to Delhi by map-reference, with the request that it be noted by the Indian military authorities.

Fortunately I had no difficulty in obtaining permission to use the factory in an emergency, together with the empty bungalows near it. I then drew up lists of those who would probably not wish to be evacuated, and planned how to distribute them among the accommodation available to us. All those who wished to stay were advised to get together and hold in readiness a stock of food, particularly children's food, drink, bedding, kerosene lamps and oil, clothing and anything else they thought they might need for a holiday in the country should we have to take one.

Thirteen British Officers held commissions in the Nizam's Army. The most senior was a retired Indian Army Brigadier who had served in a Gurkha Regiment, the most junior a young man who had been with a British Commando unit in the War. I naturally had got in touch with the Brigadier shortly after my arrival in the State, and had soon had an opportunity to meet his brother-officers also. They were extremely anxious about the course which events seemed destined to take. India was a Commonwealth country and most of them had served in the Indian Army, albeit in some cases not for long. They had no personal quarrel with India, though they deplored the way India was treating Hyderabad.

On the other hand, they had eaten the Nizam's salt—an expression with a very real meaning in India—and even if they had taken no oath of loyalty to him their duty and instinct alike urged them to earn their pay. Perhaps as important a consideration as any was the bond between them and their Hyderabadi soldiers. It was unthinkable for British officers to desert their men, and that at the very moment of battle.

My instructions were to leave the British officers in no doubt regarding the legal position. If they assisted Hyderabad in any way in hostilities against India they would be taking up arms against a Commonwealth country and thus against their own Sovereign, the Head of the Commonwealth. The several meetings at which we discussed this were as distressing to me as to them, for as a professional soldier by origin their agonising dilemma was only too obvious to me. I could only quote my instructions, and say that everyone would have to decide for himself.

Their unanimous decision, evidently taken with reluctance and after much heart-searching, was to inform the Commander of the Nizam's Army at once of the advice I had been instructed to tender to them, and to make clear that as British Subjects they would have no acceptable alternative to resigning their Hyderabadi commissions should hostilities occur. This would at least give General El-Idris an opportunity, however brief, to arrange to replace them.

I also called forthwith on the Commander, a strongly-built, soldierly Arab from the Arab community which for generations had lived in Hyderabad and served successive Nizams. We had met two or three times before and I had formed a high regard for him. He said he understood the difficult position in which the British officers found themselves and had no feeling of resentment about their decision. We had a couple of drinks and discussed the apparently inevitable course of events. He and his men would fight, he assured me. It would not be altogether a walk-over for the Indians, but he knew very well that his small force of Infantry could not hope even to delay, still less to hold, them.

My report to Government on the Hyderabadi affair will no doubt be made available to me in the Foreign and Commonwealth Relations Office Records Department. I therefore will not go into much detail here.

Briefly, the Government of India warned the United Kingdom High Commission in Delhi in confidence that units of the Indian Army would shortly enter Hyderabad State. Times and places naturally were not disclosed. This was wirelessed in cypher to me, together with the time at which the first R.A.F. aircraft would arrive at Hyderabad airport to collect evacuees. The cryptic signals on which we had agreed were at once despatched by telegraph and telephone to the various wardens I had appointed in parts of the State which had small foreign communities in them. "Aunt Mabel arriving 1100 hours to-morrow (date). Hope you can meet."

The evacuation passed off more smoothly than I had hoped. Simultaneously, those foreign nationals who wished to remain were being brought into the Bren-gun factory by the former British officers of the Hyderabadi Army, in civilian clothes. This operation also passed off successfully, and the final count was fifty-nine, excluding Hughes and myself. We signalled lists of names to Delhi as the aeroplanes left, and then a list of those in the fort.

One person was inexplicably absent: the young ex-Commando.

Shortly before the airlift began I received a signal in code which said that the Prime Minister (Mr. Attlee) wished me to do everything possible to provide for the safety and evacuation of Mrs. Blank, last heard of living at Number 14, Infantry Lines, Trimulgherry. She was related to one of his constituents.

Mrs. Blank was not on my list of British Subjects and no-one, I thought, who had the remotest claim to British protection could by then have failed to know of my presence in Hyderabad. However, I asked one of the younger British officers to drive me in a jeep to the address given in the signal.

It proved to be in a long row of small bungalows that in palmier days had been used as Other Ranks' married quarters. Playing in the dust in its tiny compound were two Indian children, wearing nothing but grubby vests down to their middles. I asked in Urdu if Mrs. Blank lived there. They shyly answered that she did. I therefore went to the front door and knocked. It was opened by a girl whom I might have taken to be an Indian had she not been wearing a European-style cotton dress. Again I asked if Mrs. Blank lived there.

"Oh, yes", she said, "she's my Granny."

I then explained who I was and why I was there. The girl asked me to come in and introduced me to Mrs. Blank, a very plump Eurasian woman who was sitting on a truckle bed. A coloured print of King George V, in naval uniform, and Queen Mary was on the wall. The only other picture was a fading photograph of a British soldier, with a handle-bar moustache and a quiff.

Though her English was rusty she insisted on using it, eking out where necessary with Urdu. She was the relict of Corporal Albert Blank of an English County Regiment of the Line.

He had married her many years ago, in the days when a soldier might serve a decade or more at a stretch in India. They had had a child and then, shortly before his Regiment was to be transferred home—Blighty, she called it—he had died. She had not heard from his relations in England for a long time, but they were the only people who could have enquired after her.

We had a comfortable chat and a cup of tea. Fortunately the old lady and her granddaughter, the mother of the children in the compound, had no wish whatever for her to be uprooted and evacuated from Hyderabad State, or even to join my group at the Bren-gun factory. As they very sensibly declared, they were no different from anyone else living in the cantonment area of Secunderabad and so would be in no more danger than the rest. Besides, Granny had never been outside Hyderabad in her life except for a visit to Bombay. What would she do in a foreign place?

They were absolutely right, I told them. By far the best course would be for them to stay together in their own bungalow, lay in some provisions in case there were a shortage of food and keep well away from any densely-populated areas in which rioting might occur. We parted on the best of terms, all of us relieved at the decision we had so easily reached. I reported to Delhi that Mrs. Blank was well and grateful for the enquiry about her. She had no wish however to leave her home. I had agreed with her that she was too old and had been too long identified with her surroundings to be moved. Before leaving Hyderabad I looked in again on the old lady and gave her a couple of pounds of tea and, for medicinal purposes, a bottle of whisky.

Hughes and I were supposed to leave with the final batch of evacuees, but he was keen as I to stay on and see the affair through. When the evacuation was over I therefore sent a short signal to Delhi saying that I regretted we had missed the last 'plane. Moreover, we were now closing the station down for eight hours because we had had no sleep for a couple of nights and were going to bed. We would call Delhi again at such-and-such an hour.

I was not best pleased when, not long after, I was told that a Hydera-badi wanted to see me urgently.

"Huzoor Sahib", said the man. "I understand you are looking after all the white people in Hyderabad State and have collected many of them here, in the Bren-gun factory."

Yes, I said, I had come from the British High Commission in Delhi to do what I could to help British and other foreign nationals if there were fighting.

"But Sahib", he asked, "did you know that there is a white man living behind the stage at the Roxy Cinema in Secunderabad?"

I said I did not. What sort of white man was he? British? The man said he thought he was. I gave him a couple of rupees for coming out to the fort to give me this information and set off by jeep, driven by the same young officer, for the Roxy Cinema.

Next door to it I noticed that a large building was heavily protected with boards across its windows and looked almost as if it had been put into a state of siege. The door opened and out came a Chinese. I asked him who owned the house and why its windows had been boarded up. To my surprise he said that all the Chinese people in the district, forty of them, had collected there and were going to stay where they were until the present troubles were over. Obviously this was the Chinese equivalent of my Bren-gun factory fort.

I then went into the empty Cinema and made my way through debris and cobwebs behind the stage. A number of rooms were locked but the door of one was ajar. I politely knocked on it and a voice said "Come in".

Sitting in a rickety cane chair, dressed in a dirty shirt, a pair of khaki shorts, stockings and plimsoll shoes, was a middle-aged man, indisputably white. He was reading a paper-back novel with a picture of a Red Indian brave on the cover.

I apologised for intruding on him, and explained who I was. I hoped that he would let me know if there were anything I could do to assist him. The last evacuation aeroplane had gone, but still I might be able to help.

He said he had heard about me but it really had not occurred to him to get in touch with me. He was in no danger and where would he go anyway, if he were evacuated from Hyderabad? At least he had a job here, as Assistant Manager of the Cinema.

I accepted at once that he was in no danger simply because he was white. Nevertheless, food supplies might run short and there was more than a slight possibility of rioting and communal violence in which he might be caught up willy-nilly. Surely it would be no hardship for him to join the British Subjects I had gathered together at the Bren-gun factory. Obviously the Cinema would not open again until the present troubles were over.

He said he would be quite ready to do this, and packed his belongings into a cardboard box. They consisted of a few articles of thin clothing, about a dozen Wild West novels and an elderly Colt revolver, carefully oiled but without ammunition.

I put him with a British railwayman's family, father, mother and two children, who took to him as readily as he to them. In no time he was helping with the washing-up and playing games with the children.

Somerset Maugham would have made something of his rather unusual story.

Jim was an American citizen who from boyhood had been fascinated by the legend of the West. After trying a variety of jobs he had joined a Rodeo show and come to India with it. When in due course it moved on, he stayed in Calcutta. Among other things he had been the Manager of Gunboat Jack, a negro boxer. Jack had followed the Rodeo into oblivion.

Jim had continued to make a living of sorts on the fringe of show-business. He had been the Agent of an itinerant concert party, then had been connected with a night-club in Bombay. Unfortunately but perhaps inevitably he had always gone down in status and pay, never up. Now he was little more than odd-job man in the Cinema, living from hand to mouth at bare subsistence level.

I told him I should have to report particulars of him to the United States Embassy in Delhi, and asked if he had any relations or close friends in the States who might welcome news of him. He could think of no-one likely to be at all interested in him, except possibly his Masonic Lodge; but he had not been in touch with it for many years.

This link with his past seemed distinctly better than nothing; once a Mason, always a Mason. I therefore included mention of the Lodge in my wireless signal to Delhi.

The High Commission signalled back that the American Embassy were very pleased to know of Jim's existence and hoped I would be able to keep him with me until they could arrange to look after him. This they would do as soon as possible.

They were as good as their word. The first civilian aeroplane into Hyderabad when communications were eventually restored brought with it an American Vice-Consul. His instructions were to conduct Jim to Madras and thence to pack him off by an American Airline to the States with the minimum delay and, I gathered, whether Jim wanted to go or not.

No doubt the Embassy was right. Down-and-nearly-outs such as Jim, however undismayed and even content they are in penury abroad, can be successfully taken care of only in their own countries. There is the question also of national prestige. No responsible Government wishes to incur the stigma of allowing one of its citizens to die in a foreign gutter.

Nevertheless, Jim plainly had no wish to leave India. The look of distress in his eyes as we shook hands before the Vice-Consul took him away made me feel I had somehow let him down.

That ending of Jim's adventures in India lay in the future. Meanwhile the Indian Army's advance into the State went inexorably on.

Details will be filled in from my report to Government on the Hyderabad affair.

Briefly, after a few days of unequal fighting, hardly more than skirmishing, the Nizam capitulated. In a short speech broadcast by the State Radio Station he declared that the mistaken policies which had led to the conflict had been forced upon him by his Government. He had never approved them. On the contrary he welcomed the action which the Delhi Government had taken and rejoiced that the way was now open for Hyderabad State to adhere to India.

The British officers and I listened together in the Bren-gun factory to this astonishing repudiation of his own Government, in effect no more than officials whom he had appointed and to whom his word was law. "Put not your trust in princes" inevitably was the disgusted soldiers' verdict. They reasoned that he had deliberately ordered, or at least allowed, his puny force of Infantry to deploy in front of the over-whelmingly stronger Indian Army in the unjustified hope that the Delhi Government would retract. When they did not, to save bloodshed he should have surrendered and abdicated. Better still of course would have been his acceptance, before hostilities began, of the plain fact that there could be only one outcome to the affair.

Indian losses were negligible. Those of the Hyderabad Army amounted to some one thousand, four hundred killed and wounded. Of the reportedly ferocious Razakars, said to have been terrorizing the countryside and to be prepared to fight to the end, little if anything was seen. I am bound to say that from the moment I entered the State the only Razakars I had come across were a few groups of men in civilian clothes, probably ex-soldiers, some of whom were drilling with shotguns and an assortment of other firearms, none dangerous at a distance, while the rest were digging trenches at places as pointless as most of those at which we used to have to dig trenches at the R.M.C., Sandhurst.

I went out to watch the leading Indian column come in and was interested to find that it was headed by our old friends and linked Regiment, the 1st (formerly King George's Own) Gurkhas. The men were laughing and joking together as usual and displaying that same rustic curiosity about new surroundings which Gurkha soldiers always show.

Major-General "Muchu" Chaudhri, sometime of the 16th Light Cavalry, was commanding the Indian Division. We had been contemporaries at the R.M.C. I called on him at his Headquarters as soon as he had settled in. He invited me to stay to dinner and I gladly accepted.

He had been pursued down the road, he said, by a string of messages from Delhi sent at the request of the U.K. High Commission. The first had given him details of the air-evacuation, and the last in the series had quoted a map-reference of the place in which I had collected my flock. All had exhorted him to take every precaution against our being put in any kind of jeopardy. Had I not come to see him he would probably have visited me, to satisfy the Government of India and the High Command that we had come to no harm.

More seriously, he explained that he done his best to avoid close fighting. His advance had been deliberately slow and his Artillery had fired around rather at positions occupied by the State Infantry. Together with a show of armour, this had sufficed more often than not to cause the Hyderabadis to withdraw. He was confident that the operations could not have been carried through with fewer casualties.

Obviously Muchu had a good many things to attend to and I therefore did not stay long. As I was taking my leave and thanking him for an excellent meal, he said "By the way, Bunny, on the way in we scooped up one of your chaps".

"Dead or alive?" I asked, trying to look as if I did not know what he was talking about. The most likely explanation of the failure of the young ex-Commando British officer of the State Army to report with his colleagues at the Bren-gun factory was that he had been killed or captured right at the start of the fighting. "Just concussed", said Muchu.

It later transpired that the young man had been out with a bridge-demolition unit when the Indian forces were entering the State and his jeep had met with a serious accident in the general confusion of the retreat from the frontier. Unconscious but otherwise unhurt he had been taken prisoner.

I told Muchu that I was sure the young man had had every intention of joining his colleagues and me at the Bren-gun factory. All of us had agreed on this, and it must have been sheer bad luck that had prevented him from getting there. I asked that he be handed over to me.

Muchu replied that he had reported the incident to the Army Commander and was awaiting instructions. Raj was expected to arrive in Hyderabad the next day.

Lieutenant-General Rajendra Singh was rather older than Muchu and I. He had won the D.S.O. with the 2nd Royal Lancers in North Africa, and now was General Officer Commanding Southern Command with his headquarters at Madras.

Communal rioting and looting had begun to break out here and there in the city during the final stages of the fighting, an ugly though not unexpected development which could have led to much bloodshed and destruction. The Indian Command restored order promptly and completely. They used the old-fashioned methods of a show of military force followed by a few public floggings.

Timing is almost always of the essence. It would be a mistake to be importunate about the ex-Commando, or to press his case on Raj before he had dealt with more important matters. On the other hand, I did not wish to leave things too long. The chances of a satisfactory outcome would almost certainly be better if we could agree on something among ourselves there and then, in Hyderabad, rather than risk the intervention of more legalistic authorities.

Raj was his usual friendly self when, two or three days after his arrival in Hyderabad, I said I expected Muchu had told him of my request that the young man be handed over to me.

He replied that he had given the affair some thought and had decided that this would probably be the best course. The young man would be handed over to me, but only when I was leaving the State; he would have to remain under guard until then. Moreover, a condition of his release would have to be my acceptance of personal responsibility for seeing him on to the first suitable boat sailing from Bombay to the United Kingdom, and meanwhile for keeping him away from the Press. The legal dilemma in which the British officers of the Nizam's Army had found themselves was common knowledge, and if the story of the young man's capture came out there might be unfortunate repercussions.

I gratefully agreed. When Hughes and I left the State for Bombay a week or so later we had the ex-Commando, an agreeable young soldier, in the four-berth sleeper with us. A wireless signal to Delhi had already obtained a berth for him, and shortly after reaching Bombay we walked up the gangway of a British ship for a drink together before he sailed home.

I followed him six months later.'

9. (right) *A Gurkha soldier*
The Gurkha Museum

10. (below) *The Imperial Palace, Hyderabad*
India Office Library and Records

11. H.I.M. The Shah, 1955, with Sir Leslie Fry, on the occasion of an official visit

Chapter Six

NEW DEPARTURES, 1948-1954

On the 2nd February 1949 Leslie Fry had completed 21 years' service in India from the date of his commission as a young officer straight from R.M.C. Sandhurst. Still somewhat surprised to find himself a civilian in H.M. Foreign Service, after a war in which he had continued to regret his inability to return to soldiering, he had settled for the fact that he liked life and work abroad. The years so far in the I.P.S. and now with the United Kingdom High Commission in Delhi and Bombay had, moreover, produced rather more action and challenge than his years in the Army. He now hoped for a posting that would mean not only a change from India (as he wrote to his Uncle Charles) but even more challenge. The fact that Sir Winston Churchill so prized the worth of the men placed as Leslie was now (with the transference of power to India) that he directed that the Foreign Office should recruit them all is sufficient to show that the administrative and political experience Leslie had acquired was of significant range. But the few years that fell between his life in India and the highlight of his career, in Hungary, were to be rather spasmodic . . . and equally diverse.

To return briefly to the small cabin in which Kate Georgina, Leslie Fry's grandmother, had sailed for India almost 70 years earlier: the fortunes of the three small boys whose beds were made up in that cabin ready for their journey had also greatly differed. Young Maxwell Fry, who at the last moment had not accompanied his mother but had stayed behind in Britain, was to contract an illness that was to make him totally deaf from childhood. As a young man, he founded (with a colleague, E. Wilson), the Midland Counties Institute for the Deaf and Dumb. This was to become his life's work. As the Warwick Institute for the Deaf, the first of many branches that were to spread—and each ultimately to become autonomous—it provided a full social life for deaf people and the deaf and dumb. And Maxwell was to meet his wife Beatrice in her capacity as founder of the Ladies' Branch of the National Deaf Club (1913). Their life was from then on permanently bound up with this work, and their two daughters—Eileen and Kay, Leslie's cousins—were to follow their own careers with equal application and success.

Leslie's own father, a professional soldier, had—as mentioned in our first chapter— died very young, never recovering properly from an illness that started with the rigours of the First World War. But the third brother, Charles, was to show an extraordinary capacity for survival, and it is probable that the first voyage to India gave him an appetite for travel, and for living abroad, that became insatiable. The obituary written by a friend when he died in America at the age of 77, described him aptly as a 'World citizen'. His love for the army was however inborn, and it was at first as a soldier that he saw the world. In 1886 he joined the 2nd Scots Guards, and in 1901 he went out to China with the 1st Chinese Regiment, raising troops as a volunteer to deal with the last of the Boxer Risings. He was there on duty until 1906, and soon returned, irresistibly drawn back to China, as Staff-Lieutenant of the Shanghai Volunteer Corps, which was formed from all nationalities for the defence of the colony. His fluent Chinese (he was a superb linguist), meant later that he was of great use in World War I, when he returned to England with a contingent of young Britishers and acted as interpreter for the Chinese Battalion. Retiring at last from active service with the rank of Lieutenant-Colonel, he returned to China in 1920, where he became a leading member of both commercial and social communities, as among other things Vice-President of Vongehr-Low China Co., Ltd., and Secretary of the Hankow Race and Recreation Club. In spite of the tense situation of 1937 onwards, Charles stayed on . . . and on the day Pearl Harbour was attacked he was, inevitably, interned. Communication with his nephew Leslie—which was always lively—then became a problem, but it is the family's belief that he survived not only as the natural outcome of his strong personality and constitution, but because he spoke fluent Japanese and must have been an important prison-interpreter. Leslie himself went down to Southampton during a post-war leave in Britain to meet his Uncle Charles on his repatriation, and was astonished by the way in which he had come through the ordeal of the Japanese prisoner-of-war camps. But Charles was never to settle again, and after a brief attempt at life in England he joined his business colleagues in Beverly Hills, where the climate suited him and his life-long and new friendships (from the Vongehrs themselves to the Japanese gardener who sent flowers to his funeral service) created for him an enjoyable retirement. It is of the utmost significance that there was a life-long correspondence between Leslie Fry and his Uncle Charles, for they shared many facets of character, perhaps especially a zest for life.

In the months that followed his final return from India in June 1949, Leslie's own zeal—as applicable to his career—was to receive an injection of patience. He knew that he was now committed to service in the Foreign Office, but for the moment this meant being firmly based at home. He had been at his Surrey home for some weeks when the 'phone rang and a cool, somewhat distant voice informed him that his future was being considered. Did he, the voice asked, prefer an Economic Department, or a Geographical? This latter, the voice explained, might lead him to any part of the world and not necessarily those regions with which he was already familiar. None too sure of his qualifications in the handling of economic affairs, Leslie chose the Geographical Department, and on the 1st November found himself reporting for work in Petty France, at the Consular Department, as deputy to its Head. Three days later 'the voice' made remote contact once more. There had been a mistake. Would Leslie report the following Monday morning to Rob Scott, Head of South East Asia Department, in the main Foreign Office buildings?

Rob Scott, later to be a Commissioner General in S.E. Asia, then the first Foreign Service Officer to be permanent Secretary in the Ministry of Defence and finally the first civilian to be Commandant of the Imperial Defence College, has a record of Crown service equalled by few. In Leslie Fry's view, he was also among the least assuming of men.

After a brief talk with Rob Scott, Leslie found himself without a portfolio, so to speak, consisting of the Foreign Office interest, as distinct from that of the Commonwealth Relations Office, in the Commonwealth countries of India, Pakistan and Ceylon, together with the foreign countries of Nepal, Tibet and the French and Portuguese possessions in the sub-continent of India, of which the main territories respectively were Pondicherry and Goa. The Kashmir dispute took up as much time as any other two problems in the portfolio put together, and might have been difficult to understand by anyone coming new to it. Fortunately Leslie had a fairly intimate knowledge of the area and some comprehension of the reasons why a solution acceptable to all parties was to be well-nigh impossible to find.

In 1950 Sir Owen Dixon, a senior Australian judge, was appointed United Nations' Commissioner for the Kashmir dispute and naturally chose to begin his work by visiting India, Pakistan and Kashmir State. Before leaving New York he telegraphed to ask H.M. Government if they would supply him with someone who had experience of these places and could take care of the many administrative details that would have to be dealt with on the tour.

In the Foreign Office Leslie himself advised against putting forward any member of the former Indian Services. However obviously he busied himself with administrative matters, he would be suspected of influencing Sir Own politically. It would be better, Leslie thought, for the Commissioner to be seen coming to his task with an open mind.

However, in the Commonwealth Relations Office a proposal that he himself should be given the job had been submitted simultaneously, and was accepted.

On Sir Owen's arrival in London, they spent some hours in the Office discussing a long memorandum Leslie had prepared for him on the Kashmir problem, and dined together afterwards. Leslie assured Sir Owen that he would be delighted to go to Asia with him. He doubted, however, whether the Governments of India and Pakistan would welcome the continued presence with him of a member of the former Indian Political Service, now in the Foreign Office. It might be as well, he suggested, for him to set out alone and to consult Pandit Nehru, the first person on whom he was to call, about Leslie Fry joining him. If the reply were favourable, Leslie would be on an aeroplane for Delhi within 24 hours. Sir Owen agreed.

Almost immediately after his arrival in Delhi he telegraphed London to say that Pandit Nehru's response had been unfavourable. He had told Sir Owen that he well remembered Leslie Fry, and had no objection to him on personal grounds. But he would ask Sir Owen to take into consideration the fact that Fry had belonged to a Service generally regarded in India as composed of reactionaries who had stood in the path of the country's progress to independence.

Leslie did not join Sir Owen on his mission for the United Nations.

His long and exacting apprenticeship in the External Affairs Department of the Government of India had equipped him as well as most for demanding to see all the previous correspondence, for pushing the files around to every Department even remotely likely to be interested, for remembering that the Treasury must be consulted at each step and for the general rigours of secretariat work, including the temperament of one's boss. What it had not taught him was how to work in a noisy room cheek-to-jowl with five other, younger officers and, above all, to write practically everything out instead of dictating minutes and drafts to his own secretary.

The latter handicap was overcome fortuitously. Soon after joining the Department he had telephoned to arrange courtesy calls on the Heads of such ancillary Branches of the Office as were concerned with his own department. These included the Secretarial Services Section. Leslie duly dropped in to pay his respects to its Head. She was a trim spinster lady, alleged to have been recruited to the Foreign Office as a young shorthand-typist in the days when such ladies were protected by a screen between them and the officers from whom they were taking dictation. He liked her; she reminded him slightly of the spinster aunt who had brought him up.

After a year in South-East Asia Department Leslie Fry was transferred to Eastern Department as Assistant in it, that is to say, second-in-command. The Department dealt with the Middle East, and was one to which he was to return as its Head.

In the meantime, an important promotion came through. On 6th August 1951 Leslie was appointed Counsellor of Embassy—in military parlance second-in-command—at the British Embassy in Lisbon. In this capacity he acted as Chargé d'Affaires through the remainder of 1951 and 1952. The then Ambassador, Sir Nigel Ronald, was not a well man, and it meant that there was every need for a second-in-command who could take responsibility. *The Times'* obituary on Sir Nigel (May 16th 1973) describes him as an exceptionally clear thinker, regarded during his seven years in Lisbon as a strong and successful champion of British interests, but perhaps not always so effective in the Foreign Office, where his role was perhaps diminished by sheer intellectuality. There is no doubt that quite apart from the value in his subsequent appointments of this assumption of more than usual responsibilities in Lisbon, the example of a strong pedagogic nature at large in the post-war manipulations of diplomacy had its lessons for the up-and-coming Leslie Fry.

Life at the British Embassy at this time (it was a pleasant house, well suited to entertainment, and with a splendid garden) seems to have been particularly pleasing, and the fact that Portugal was Britain's oldest ally meant that culturally and socially there were many shared interests with the residents of the capital, and a lively interest in all things British which it befell the Embassy to continue to promote. Leslie himself was particularly active in these fields, and when in December 1952 a successful exhibition was held in the British Institute, Lisbon, to commemorate the centenary of the death of the Duke of Wellington, it was 'Mr. L. A. C. Fry, O.B.E.' who gave a detailed, both academic and lively, account of the campaign of 1810. The text of this lecture is now preserved in the annual report of the Lisbon Branch of the Historical Association, under whose auspices the entire exhibition was arranged. Among other subjects which Leslie Fry found appealed to the Portuguese was the history of English silver, on which he also lectured. And, conversely, he for his part began a study of the Portuguese language which was to stand him in good stead when he eventually was appointed as H.M. Ambassador to Brazil.

Had he lived to complete the text of his autobiography, Leslie would no doubt also have written on more serious aspects of life in Portugal, and at some length on the character and policies of the then Head of State, Professor Dr. Salazar. There was much that appealed to him in the intellectual who could also effectively enter the arena of action, and though his policies were controversial and later totally reversed, they were at first continued in essentials by Marcello Caetano, and play a major role in the studies of 20th-century Portuguese history.

On returning to London and his new appointment as Head of Eastern Department on 14th September 1953, Leslie inherited an uneasy situation in connection with relations with Iran. The Eastern Department dealt with the Middle East in general, and in this instance the 'Abadan affair' had interrupted good relations with Iran, and the British stake in Iranian oil had greatly suffered. At the same time, the Shah himself was experiencing dangerous shifts in the bid for power. The picture was very different from that which the young Leslie Fry found on his posting to the consulate in Zabul for a year and a half before the war. This was the capital of the south-eastern Province of Iran, and the consulate was paid for in moieties by H.M. Government and the Government of India, serving mainly as a listening post on the frontier between Iran and Afghanistan. No doubt, Leslie surmised in notes he made on the subject of those months in Zabul, this had been of importance when Iran (Persia, as it was then called) had been divided into two spheres of influence, Russian in the north and British in the south. But by 1936, when Leslie arrived, there was no such reason for maintaining a Consulate in Siestan and he found himself with almost nothing to do. However, there is no doubt that the leisured time there gave him to some extent an insight which proved useful when it came to the handling of the problems of 15 years later.

As far back as two years before Leslie's appointment, the 'Abadan affair' had come to a head, with the seizure by Iranian troops of the Abadan refinery, which was from then on closed to almost all British workers. Two years later Leslie still had to take into consideration lack of willingness on the part of the American government to encourage or enjoin any exercise Britain might undertake to protect her interests. When the United Nations Security Council met to consider the matter, it was Mossadequ, whom the Shah himself considered to be a danger to the stabilisation of a modern Iranian state, who subtly warned the Council not to come to any decisions that would constitute a danger to international peace. Britain was effectively warned off, in October 1952 diplomatic relations with Iran were severed, and a year later the bid to restore her interests was still ineffective. And the duel between the Shah and his Prime Minister was out in the open, crowned by an attempted coup in 1953, by which time the Shah had already, at Mossadequ's bidding, transferred most of his wealth to the Government, and certainly all of his actual powers to Mossadequ himself. But by June 1953 America was showing unwilling to concede Mossadequ's appeal for loans until the oil dispute was settled. Resistance to Mossadequ was by them also accelerating at home, and the coup and counter-coup that were to bring him down brought the Shah from a helpless, miserable exile in Rome. And in February 1955 Leslie went by train to Southampton to escort a reinstated Shah to London for an official visit that was to signpost improved relations. The Abadan dispute, which had so nearly crippled British Petroleum (known then as the Anglo-Iranian Oil Company) and at the same time threatened Iran's own ability to sell its oil, is now acknowledged to have been a watershed in the post-war story of the world's oil industry.

It was in the second year of his appointment as Head of Eastern Department in the Foreign Office in London that Leslie met and married Penelope Bentley Bentley, only daughter of the late Norman Wilson Bentley, of Pannal Hall, near Harrogate. The wedding took place on 17 September 1954, at Caxton Hall, followed by a blessing in Holy Trinity, Brompton.

Chapter Seven

HUNGARY, 1956

By Lieut.-Colonel Noel Cowley

History has been written in a number of accounts of the Hungarian uprising in 1956; it is not the intention now to write history, but to give a more personal narrative of events in Hungary, and to convey the observations as seen from the British Legation of those tempestuous times.

In 1955 Leslie Fry was appointed H.M. Minister Plenipotentiary to Hungary and travelled with his wife to Budapest to take up the post on 24th October. He looked forward to his new position with intense interest, as not only was it his first appointment as head of one of H.M. Government's Overseas Missions, but it was also one which he anticipated would be full of political activity, and would provide an opportunity to observe a Communist régime at close quarters. However, little did he think that he would become a central witness of, and a key figure in, a major European revolution.

The ceremony of the presentation of credentials was arranged as quickly as possible, so that the new Minister and his wife might attend the large reception which was to be held at the Soviet Embassy to mark the anniversary of the Great October Socialist Revolution of 1917, which is always celebrated by the Soviet Union on 7th November.

The presentation of his Letter of Credence was, of course, made to the President, István Dobi, a figurehead who lived in an alcoholic haze. He was accompanied by the Prime Minister, Hegedüs, another cipher. The effective power in the country was, however in the hands of Mátyás Rákosi, First Secretary of the Hungarian Communist Party, who was said to be Stalin's most apt pupil. He ruled with an iron hand, using all the devices of his master—terror, torture and oppression to the full. Rákosi had at his control the dreaded State Secret police. This Force was called Allamvedelmi Osztály (AVO), State Security Section, but it was later re-named Allamvedelmi Hivatal (AVH), meaning State Security Office, but the old infamous name of AVO could not be suppressed and it continued to be known generally by that name.

For a foreigner fully to absorb the situation in Communist Hungary it is necessary to understand the penetrating influence of the AVO., which permeated every aspect of life—they were here, they were there, they were everywhere. They were supreme in power over the other forces of the State, even over the Government itself, and were answerable only to the Party leadership. The role of this force is vital to the very existence of the Communist State—any Communist state—as rule is by decree carried out by force if necessary, and the views of the people are irrelevant. Only if the people can raise a force capable of challenging the rule of the State will their views be taken into account.

The 'AVO' was a military-type force with military uniforms and ranks, and was thought to number about 30,000. It was a separate entity divorced from the orthodox 'blue police' and from the other armed services. To enable it to carry out its insidious tasks much of it operates in civilian clothes. In addition to its regular members there were thousands of informers, the vast majority of whom were involuntary and were drawn in by fear of reprisals on themselves or their families if they failed to respond to the demands made on them. It was well known in diplomatic circles that all local employees of foreign diplomatic Missions were required to report at frequent intervals to the AVO for interrogation.

Many of the men of this secret police were little more than animals whose brutality knew no limits, and whose bestiality in torturing their hapless fellow countrymen can only be equalled by their big brothers of the Russian KGB and the barbaric hordes of early European history.

They excelled in the task of pouncing on any individual who mis-guidedly, or by mischance, might have made an anti-Communist remark or who perhaps was found with western books or literature, however politically innocent.

The AVO often carried out its arrests in the early hours of the morning, and the vans used for this purpose have been observed at 3 a.m. or 4 a.m. at this gruesome work. One instance was known when the AVO went to a house at this time, arrested the husband and wife and took them away, leaving two young children asleep and alone in the house to wake up in the morning to find their parents gone, probably never to see them again.

The AVO also had the task of the surveillance of Western diplomats, which entailed watching all their movements and often the movements of their families, tapping their telephones and planting listening devices in their homes whenever the opportunity occurred. Indeed, it seemed that the aim was to penetrate areas of family life. An occasion is well known of a listening microphone being hidden between the twin beds of a Western diplomat and his wife.

The pertinacity of these gentlemen is well illustrated by an occasion when a foreign Military Attaché was entertaining some senior Hungarian Army officers to dinner in his house. The evening went well, innocent of any political exchanges, and the Hungarian officers clearly enjoyed them-selves singing a number of their Army songs. In the later course of the evening, a Hungarian General asked a locally-engaged waiter to bring another bottle of wine. The waiter told him in no uncertain terms that he could have no more wine and that he, in the waiter's view, had had enough. The particular waiter worked frequently at diplomatic functions in the capital, and his action on this occasion served to support the suspicions of many Western diplomats that he was an AVO man.

There were several reasons for this tight 'policing' and supervision of members of the Western Corps Diplomatique. One was routine espionage to try to learn what Western governments were thinking and doing; another, to discover any indiscretions, of whatever nature, in which any of these members might have become involved, in order that they might be used to blackmail them into divulging secret material. Further, also, to track down local people, either making contact with Western missions, or who might be approached by them. Any Hungarian who spoke to a Western diplomat without official reason was immediately under suspicion and would henceforth be watched or called in for interrogation. Western diplomats knew the risks that local people ran in this respect, and generally avoided making friends with them so as not to compromise them.

The exercise of this supervision meant frequently following the diplomats and their families when they moved about Budapest or travelled in the provinces. The method of following people sometimes varied, and it was observed that the 'tail', as it was called, when in the open countryside would on occasions travel five or 10 minutes behind the car under observation. It was thought that the purpose of this interval was to provide an opportunity for the travellers to make contact with local people, thus allowing the AVO to arrive on the scene and identify the locals concerned. Wives would be followed when shopping and a Security Policeman would stand in the shop.

One aspect of the intrusion by the Security Police, into the lives of Western diplomats, was the tapping of telephones, and this was regarded as a permanent feature of life.

It was in this slightly macabre atmosphere of the ever-prevailing shadow of this sinister presence that Leslie Fry and his wife were to live for the next few years. Away from the official bureaucratic circle they found the Hungarians a charming and friendly people, with a natural sense of politeness, courtesy and vivaciousness, showing a well-developed humour and an awareness of history and culture. There was a touch of the dramatic in their character which was exemplified by their love and deep knowledge of Shakespeare, sometimes to the embarrassment of less well-versed English friends.

The Hungarians, the Magyars (pronounced with a soft 'g'), migrated from the more inner areas of Russia in the ninth century, finally settling in the fertile valley of the Danube. They have a volatile fiery nature, acting with a quickness of spirit which leads them at times to act first and think afterwards, which is probably how they came to build such a reputation as great cavalry soldiers—the English word 'hussar' being derived from the Hungarian word 'huszár'. There is a word in the Hungarian language, developed since the 19th century, used to portray this quality, which is 'virtus', a Latin expression approximating to the French 'bravoure' or 'panache'. Fortunately they have a providential fortitude in adversity which serves them well in difficult times, and their sense of humour is never far below the surface.

The nation has had a stormy history which may partly account for a philosophical outlook. In the present situation of occupation by Russian forces and rule from Moscow, they are inclined to point to the fact that they were occupied by Turkey for some 200 years, and yet survived with their national spirit and character intact.

Over the past century there has been a dilution, particularly in the capital city Budapest, of German, Austrian and a few other European races, leading to a more mixed population, but the national characteristics of the Magyars predominate with a sense of patriotism which prevails through all attempts by their Soviet masters to suppress it.

Late 1955 was the aftermath of the great Geneva Conference and the spirit of co-existence lapped around the diplomatic communities of East and West, and Leslie Fry saw this as an opportunity to press for information about the many British subjects, and Hungarian members of the British Legation, who had disappeared over the years of the Communist régime. Complete ignorance of this would invariably be expressed, but the occasion sometimes lead to a more formal interview when Leslie Fry would pull from his pocket a complete list of these missing people which he would put before the official concerned. During a private talk with the President of Hungary in an adjacent room after the Presentation of Credentials ceremony, Leslie Fry put this list of missing persons in front of him asking for vigorous enquiries to be made.

Andropov, the Soviet Ambassador, who was later to play a prominent part in the Hungarian uprising, had been a senior official during the Second World War at some Soviet port where his job had been to receive British naval convoys. His knowledge of English was very fair, and the only difficulty in talking with him was that he was never prepared to discuss anything of political, economic or topical importance. He restricted his conversation to the arts, particularly literature. On being asked who his favourite, more or less modern, English author was—expecting the stock answer of Dickens to be given—to some astonishment Andropov replied 'Oscar Wilde'. He explained that he preferred him to other writers because he described a small circle of society so clearly. It was by no means a superficial comment.

The new Minister and his wife were quickly caught up in the busy, at times almost exhausting, life of the diplomatic circle; the social-cum-official round was never ceasing, which was surprising in a way when it is considered that East and West Missions never exchanged social visits, and social intercourse between Western diplomats and private Hungarian citizens was impractical—the AVO saw to that.

On occasion the Hungarian Foreign Ministry organised outings for the members of foreign Diplomatic Missions. These were usually arranged in groups according to status. Some shooting parties were organised which provided a good day's shooting, usually on the 'puszta'; the extensive open flat grass plains of central Hungary where, up to the Second World War, horse-breeding took place on a considerable scale and large herds of wild horses roamed freely. The method of conducting these shoots was somewhat different from those customary in England. The guns, each with a beater/guide would walk out to form an enormous circle; the guns would then walk to converge on the centre. This operation was carried out four or five times in the day usually resulting in a good bag of pheasant, partridge and hare. The groups for these parties were usually drawn from either the Heads of Diplomatic Missions, Service Attachés or other diplomatic staff. The outings composed of the Service Attachés were comparatively safe—after all it was reasonable to expect that the majority of them had handled guns before, but those consisting of the Heads of Missions were, perhaps, not quite so free from the element of surprise. It is not recorded in the game book, but it was reported that one Ambassador 'winged' a colleague from another country by scoring a neat hit in the legs.

The genial spirit of the Geneva Conference between the Communists and the West prevailed through the summer of 1956. The summer weather was good and escape from the exacting diplomatic merry-go-round was found in the lovely countryside, which varied from the Danube itself to the Hungarian riviera of Lake Nalaton and to the hills of the mountainous regions. Unfortunately, the countryside was sometimes marred by ugly modern barracks, surrounded by high wire fences with sentries posted; frequently the barracks were occupied by Soviet troops. Near a frontier the grimness of the conditions of life in the country was impressed on the traveller by the almost ceaseless surveillance of the area by high watch-towers. These were built on stilts some 40 or 50 feet from the ground and were close enough together for one to be always in sight. The atmosphere in those areas of a concentration camp, or prisoner-of-war camp, could not be escaped. The road from Budapest to Vienna, for a time, runs alongside the Danube which forms the frontier with Czecho-slovakia, and on the Czech side these grisly watch-towers line the bank. On the frontier with Austria the additional presence of minefields made the gruesome feeling of being trapped even sharper.

The wives of Western diplomats carried out their domestic shopping in Budapest where there was a large central market with excellent country produce of a very high quality, but often on these occasions a wife would be trailed by AVO security men who would even follow her into a shop to watch what she purchased and to check that the shopkeeper engaged in no bourgeois activities nor made any non-official contact. On one occasion, taking the dogs for an airing, Mrs. Fry noticed that she was being tailed and decided to give the Secret Police a good walk for their money. She took three hours over it.

In June, Leslie Fry held the customary reception to celebrate the anniversary of the birthday of Her Majesty the Queen. The weather was superb, and the party took place on the verandah and in the gardens of the Minister's residence and was attended by some 900 people, some of whom, being expatriate British subjects, welcomed such an opportunity to display their loyalty to their Sovereign and country; probably the only time in the year they had a chance to do this. Members of other Diplomatic Missions were also invited, as were the leading figures in the Government. In a Communist country, who will attend from the Government is always a matter of speculation and is not known until the figures themselves arrive. It can depend on a number of factors; what the political situation happens to be at that moment, who is in favour or out of favour in the Party, or, perhaps, the personal relationship between the Minister and the leading members of the Government. It was a mark of Leslie Fry's personal qualities and diplomatic abilities that, in the short time he had been in Budapest, he had established a first-class rapport with the Communist Government for, on the occasion, the Party Leaders attended headed by no less than Mátyás Rákosi himself in genial smiling bonhomie; indeed, can the most lethal of tigers smile?

During the height of the summer of 1956 the voice of opposition to the Communist régime in Hungary began to be heard and gradually to come out more into the open. Under the pressure the 'mistakes' of the Stalin era were openly admitted by the Soviet Party leaders. News broke at the time that Kruschev, at the 20th Congress of the Soviet Union Communist Party, had denigrated Stalin and expressed the opinion that there was more than one road to Socialism. In Hungary the intelligentsia, the writers, the authors, the poets, the journalists, have always played a considerable role; they took this up and, naturally, began to write more stimulating articles than they had produced before and there were a good many demands, for example by the students, that there should be more Hungarian identity. In the middle of July, Anastas Mikoyan, Soviet Deputy Premier, visited Hungary and persuaded Mátyás Rákosi that it was time for him to retire—he was an anachronism. There was something like a couple of days argument but eventually Rákosi went, and it is thought that the very first mistake that was made by the Soviet Union was the appointment, in Rákosi's place, of his closest lieutenant Ernö Gerö. Shortly after this there was a meeting in the Crimea of the Russian leaders, President Tito and Ernö Gerö. This was intended to kiss and make up after the breach with the Soviet Union by Tito and to show that all was now well. The Communist Party of Hungary was invited to send a delegation to Yugoslavia. Much about that time the Poles began to grow restive, but in the event, they did not revolt in any way; probably largely to the influence of Cardinal Wyszinski. However, in Hungary, this debate continued about a separate road to Socialism. At this time the difference in the national characteristics of the Hungarian people from those surrounding them began to emerge. The Magyars have a very long history behind them; a very different history of oppression, and they and the Poles have always regarded themselves as the eastern bastions of Western civilisation. For example, in 1848, when the Hungarians revolted against the Hapsburgs, they were suppressed by a Russian army, but it is of considerable significance that Polish sympathy lay with the Hungarians, and General Bem, a Polish general, fought with distinction on the Hungarian side and became a national hero to the Hungarian people.

In considering the progression of events at this time and whether the real revolutionary emotions had been developing for a long time, or whether it was something that arose quickly in the few months beforehand, an authoritative view is that it arose remarkably quickly, although there had for years been a sense of deep frustration. Hungary has a natural agricultural economy and, of course, Marxism, Leninism and Communism demand an industrial proletariat, and this can hardly come about unless there is some industry to generate it. So Hungary was wrenched away from an agricultural economy to an unnatural industrial one, which meant, for instance, the building of the new town and complex Sztalinváros by many thousands of people who were involuntarily pressed into service and told, virtually overnight, to pack a grip and report at such and such a railway station to go and help build this new steelworks. In addition, a strongly-guarded heavy industrial site was built on the island of Csepel, a large island about 30 miles long in the Danube south of Budapest. As events turned out, this traumatic reorganisation to impose heavy industry proved to be a dismal failure, and the shambles and chaos of the attempts to administer the plan were, in numerous cases, quite astonishing. There were, certainly, other major causes of dissatisfaction which contributed to the general state of turmoil but, although the events in the middle of October were regarded by Western observers as of no little significance, and must surely have caused some very worried concern amongst the Communist Party leaders, there was no thought that an armed revolt would build up; such an idea would have been met with dismay by the average Hungarian in the street, and was not under contemplation by the student groups pressing for greater freedom.

In the second half of October meetings of the student groups, the intellectuals and the writers circles became rather more pronounced and the demands of these groups on the Government became more persistent. The students, in a 16-point declaration, called for far-reaching and fundamental reorganisation of the Government, political attitudes, the economy and social ideals. The first of these demands, which was clearly of great importance to them, was for the removal of all Soviet troops from Hungary. They called for democratic election of Communist Party leaders and officials of the Government. The removal and trial of Rákosi and other Stalinist Party men for crimes they were alleged to have committed during the Stalin era was included amongst these points. So also was the return to lead the country of Imre Nagy, a man of rural stock, a dedicated Communist of many years' standing. He was a humanist and a man of the people, and with little doubt the most popular leader in the country. A former Prime Minister, his human and more tolerant ways had led him into conflict with Kruschev, resulting in his relegation to obscurity; at least, to as much obscurity as a man of his popularity would allow, but this was not as complete as the Stalinist Communist leaders of Hungary would have wished. Also included in the students' 16 points were demands for political and economic equality within the Soviet Bloc, control and commercial marketing of the country's uranium deposits, and an enquiry into the concessions granted to the Russians in this respect, a review of all political trials and the release of innocent people, the right to strike and the replacement in the national flag of the Soviet insignia by the traditional Hungarian Arms of Kossuth.

The demands by the students, together with the demands by the intellectuals and authors for less repression and more freedom of expression, although made well within the ideals and doctrines of Communism, were anathema to the Government leaders who held power by force and not by democratic mandate.

Against this background the day of 23rd October, 1956, opened with the general population going about their business in the normal way, but events began moving quickly as the day wore on. Public meetings of students took place and a march was arranged through Budapest. This march was at first made up of students, but it was quickly joined by people of all descriptions—men of all walks of life, women and children and members of the armed forces, in all building up to many thousands. It was observed from the British Legation as it made its way along one of the opposite sides of the square.

On this day Leslie Fry and his wife were fulfilling an engagement at a Government scientific laboratory about five miles out of Budapest. This had been regarded as an unprecedented distinction, and the invitation had been made in response to a cocktail party which had been given at the British Legation, at which a number of Hungarian scientists had been shown a Central Office of Information film on British nuclear energy installations. The Director of the Laboratory had received much of his training at Liverpool University, had married an Englishwoman and had moved to the Irish Republic on the outbreak of war in 1939. A committed Communist, he had returned to Hungary after the war and was then one of the leading scientists in the country. On the way out of the city interest had been aroused when several columns of people, men, women and children, were observed walking along in an orderly and purposeful manner. It was assumed they were going to a funeral, for those leading each column were carrying wreaths and, if that assumption had been correct, clearly it must have been someone of considerable official importance. Not only because so many mourners were involved, but because the authorities would not normally countenance an assembly of more than a handful of people. However, enlightenment was soon to follow that the gatherings they had witnessed were the first public demonstrations, which were to erupt without conscious design into the Hungarian nation's struggle for freedom. The columns marching to the city were converging on the statue of General Bem near the Ministry of Foreign Affairs. It seemed appropriate that, as the Polish General had fought with the Hungarians in their revolt against the Hapsburg rulers of Austria-Hungary in 1848, they should now be expressing their sympathy with the Polish people who were stirring against a latter-day Russian Imperialism, and where better than at the historic monument to Bem?

The Director and his senior assistant of the Laboratory welcomed their British guests and after a cup of coffee, began to show the complicated apparatus with which they were conducting their experiments. Twenty minutes or so later the Director was called to the telephone; when he came back he drew his assistant aside, spoke a few words to him, and expressed his apologies saying that he had been summoned to the Ministry in Budapest and would have to leave immediately. The assistant continued the tour, but it quickly became apparent that he was preoccupied and it was sensed that it would be politic to conclude the visit; it was obvious that for whatever reason the warmth with which the visit had started had evaporated, and an indication that another engagement was imminent was greeted with evident relief.

On returning to the city outskirts after leaving the Laboratory, it became abundantly clear that some momentous event was taking place. People everywhere were hurrying to the main square of the city and, indeed, Petöfi Square, named after a hero poet of the 1848 Revolution, was almost full. The least responsive of observers could not have failed to sense the atmosphere of tension and excitement. In the serious circumstances which were obviously arising Leslie Fry drove straight to the Legation and Mrs. Fry walked back to the Residence in Buda on the west side of the Danube. On the west side is Buda where the Castle Hill rises on which stands the old Royal Palace, and beyond that is the main residential area; to the east of the river lies Pest, containing the business, commercial and industrial centres; communication between the two halves is dependent on several bridges spanning the river. The British Legation was in Pest, but a large number of the families of the Legation staff lived in Buda.

Several aspects of the day of 23rd October were, to some extent, obscured by confusion, and the Government itself seemed to be in some turmoil. At students meetings on 22nd October it had been decided that the youth of Budapest would hold a silent demonstration of sympathy in front of the Embassy of the Polish Peoples' Republic. It was the aim of the demonstration to express the deep sympathy and solidarity of youth with the events in Poland. They avowed that the demonstration of sympathy would take place in the spirit of Socialist democracy and promised to maintain order and discipline.

This was supported by the Hungarian Writers' Union which expressed its accord with the events in Poland. Hungarian writers, who in the course of the past years had constantly fought against Rákosi's policies and for democratisation, believed the chief tasks of the Hungarian public were: firstly, to ensure further advance on the part of Socialist democracy; and, secondly, to avoid enthusiasm for the events in Poland provoking the Hungarian workers and students into disturbing their happiness and political endeavours.

However, a decree from the Minister of the Interior was broadcast on the radio banning any public meetings or demonstrations but, realising that this ban had exacerbated the situation and would be ignored anyway, some two hours later it was withdrawn.

At this time Ernö Gerö, who was visiting Yugoslavia, returned hurriedly and broadcast to the nation in the late afternoon. His speech greatly disappointed the Hungarian people. He said that there must be no loosening of the ties with the Soviet Union and that everyone must go home and give up the demonstrations. The speech, which was brusque and obliquely offensive to the Hungarian people's genuine endeavours, did much to irritate the feelings of the thousands of demonstrators by this time massed in the city. Many Western observers believe this speech did much to further the Revolution, and it showed clearly Gerö's inept remoteness from the real situation and complete lack of understanding of the feelings of the people.

On the edge of the city park in a vast open square stood an enormous bronze figure of Stalin about 20 feet high, mounted about 40 feet high on a long concrete plinth of the nature of Lenin's tomb in Moscow. One of the students' 16 demands had been for the removal of this statue, which was regarded as a symbol of Stalinist tyranny and political oppression, and for its replacement by a monument to the memory of the martyred fighters for freedom of 1848. During the course of the evening a very large proportion of the crowd surged towards the monument and began to take matters into their own hands. Ropes were attached to the statue and attempts made to pull it down; at one time trolley-buses were hooked to the ropes, but the enormous bronze figure resisted all assault until some resourceful members of the community arrived on the scene with oxy-acetylene burners. After the application of these to the knee joints the figure of Stalin crashed to the ground, to the vast roar of approval from the extensive and delighted crowd.

By this time in the evening the spirits of the population were up and the dash and emotional patriotism of the Magyars had been kindled; the whole of Budapest was infected by this intense atmosphere of revolt against Russian oppression and domination.

Delegations of student leaders went to the Budapest radio station for the purpose of having their demands broadcast over the national radio, but by that time the building was in a state of armed siege, heavily protected by armed AVO troops, and the students were refused entry or even a hearing by the Director.

The Minister and staff of the Legation were alert to these develop-ments, and some were out and about to discover what was going on. The Third Secretary of the Legation, Mark Russell, observed the events in Bem Square and at the Petőfi monument. The crowds were converging on the latter in an obviously emotional, indeed at times almost hysterical, state. In Bem Square the crowd swelled to enormous proportions, and loudspeakers were calling upon the people to rally around the student leaders who had drafted the now well-known 16-point demands.

Since the Communist takeover of Hungary the national tricolour flag of red, white and green had had imposed on it the Soviet insignia of the hammer and sickle. By the time these events were taking place the flag began appearing with the hammer and sickle cut out, leaving only the national colours of Hungary. Soon this symbol of patriotism was being displayed from the windows of buildings in the city.

At the nearby barracks, which was in a stage of siege, the crowd were calling on the soldiers to join their cause. It was obvious that they had caught the mood of the occasion and were ready to join the demonstra-tion, had they not been barred by their commander. Already amongst the crowd was a considerable number of Army officers, some of quite high rank, who gave encouragement to the soldiers in the barracks. It was learned later that the soldiers, after draping the new cut-out flag from their barracks, joined the crowds which were also swollen by a Polish students' contingent and a large party of workers from the industrial plants of Csepel Island. In this atmosphere of exhilaration the spirit of national identity, pride and patriotism knew no bounds; the old Hungarian National Anthem was constantly being sung and at all times being hummed by those around. For years during the Communist rule no-one in Hungary had really dared to laugh openly, for the only interpretation which the authorities placed on it was that it was mockery or disapproval of the system, but now the crowd were laughing just for the joy of laughing. It was a state of morale for which any general before battle would pray with all the fervour his soul could muster.

The main activities of the demonstrators centred around the Budapest radio station, where the students pressed ever harder for their demands to be broadcast and for the radio station to be in the hands of the people and not at the control of the Party. It was a state of confrontation and it was here that the first shots of the Revolution were fired by the AVO, and fatal casualties were sustained by the unarmed demonstrators. Some Hungarian tanks, sent by the Ministry of Defence to disperse the demonstrators, arrived, but the soldiers in them went over to the side of the demonstrators, and the Major who had commanded them was shot by the AVO. These devasting events caused the crowds to overrun the natural bounds of restraint; until that time the demonstrators had been unarmed, but, now in the fury of the circumstances, arms began appearing among them. They were obtained initially from the soldiers who, almost en masse, refused to fire on their own people and joined their struggle. Later other sources came into operation; the workers from the arms factories on Csepel Island soon brought arms to the scene, and the demonstrators raided the Secret Police headquarters and obtained further arms there.

The fighting between the demonstrators and the AVO continued throughout the night, mainly centred around the radio station. Some of the Legation British staff tried to keep track of what was was going on. The Military Attaché was out all night, mainly watching events around the radio station, returning to his house in Buda at about 3.30 a.m. for a change into more practical clothes and some breakfast. Returning to the city at about 4.30 a.m. he met up with a column of Russian tanks driving into Budapest. From time to time they were loosing off bursts of machine-gun fire, apparently at nothing in particular, but probably intended to frighten the inhabitants.

Early on the morning of 24th October, Leslie Fry and his staff set about assessing the situation. No-one was in any doubt that the peaceful demonstrations of the previous day had now developed into a major uprising, and that the population had the bit between its teeth and there was no holding it. The initial reaction was one of exhilaration and excitement, as clearly it was a historical moment in the long, eventful history of Hungary, and there was a deep sense of privilege in being there to witness it. However, all were aware that the job of diplomats was not to become involved in the fighting; the main task was to report to the British Government what was going on.

The Legation was fortunate in receiving a good amount of information; the telephone was still operating and throughout the British members of the staff quietly went about observing events. It was known that the Russians had armoured formations stationed in Hungary and it seemed clear that elements of these had driven into Budapest in some hurry during the night to no concerted plan; they drove to the main centres where they had hoped to deal with the demonstrators. In all probability they had counted on their presence, accompanied by some threatening bursts of machine-gun fire, frightening the population into a submission of their exuberance. Nothing could have been farther from reality; the intervention of the Russians only seemed to make the people more angry, and more determined to pursue the fight.

The protests and demonstrations before 23rd October had been aroused by a deep feeling of hostility to the conduct of affairs by the Communist Government of the country, but the transition of events into an armed uprising was, without doubt, spontaneous and brought about by a combination of a number of different incidents which both angered the people and engendered a fervour of national spirit and patriotism.

From the bloody fracas at the radio building, armed groups of what had now become known as Freedom Fighters established themselves, and centres of resistance built in numerous parts of Pest, the main bastions being the famous Kilián barracks and some adjacent areas around. However, there was no central command, and co-ordination between the groups appeared to be non-existent in any general sense; each seemed to be fighting its own battle, determined to resist to the end.

This lack of central command probably served the Freedom Fighters in good stead as there was no operational centre for the Russians to eliminate; each point of resistance had to be dealt with individually, and some were pretty elusive.

The fighting during the day of 24th October spread across the river to Buda from Pest and the bridges over the Danube connecting the two became unusable. This meant that many of the staff in the Legation were cut off from their families in Buda, and they prepared to camp the night in their offices, not thinking at that time that it would be some six weeks before they would be able to return to live in their own homes.

The Government of Hungary by this time was clearly in a state of turmoil and apparent impotence. Hegedüs, the Prime Minister, was replaced by Imre Nagy, it seems as a gesture to the people in the hope that his presence in authority would calm them. Nagy appealed to the nation to lay down their arms and to cease fighting, and he promised as soon as possible the systematic democratisation of the country in every field of Party, State, political and economic life. This appeal went unheeded, and it was clear that the Hungarian Army and 'blue' police were quickly going over to the side of the people, leaving only the Secret Police to resist. The AVO had no alternative but to fight in order to defend itself.

Through the course of the next four or five days fierce and bitter fighting was waged by the Freedom Fighters against the Russian forces and against the AVO. The Freedom Fighters were made up of men, women, boys and girls of a considerable range of ages, occupations and interests; but all, with no prior briefing or exhortation, seemed to have the same telepathic purpose: a freedom to have a democratic say in their destiny, and freedom from the yoke and oppression of the Soviet control and occupation of their country. Youngsters, boys and girls of an age of 12 or 14, were armed and taking part in this struggle.

At an early stage in the uprising it was reported to the Legation that two British subjects were marooned in an hotel in the middle of Pest. The British Consul, Joan Fish, on informing Leslie Fry, declared that it was a Consular duty to look after individual British subjects and, therefore, proposed to go to the hotel to retrieve them. Leslie Fry agreed that, ordinarily, it was indeed the Consul's responsibility to look after individual British subjects, but he considered that the circumstances were not altogether ordinary. There were unmistakable political considerations which made it desirable for him to attend to the matter himself. This did not satisfy the Consul who argued hotly that Leslie was metaphorically holding her skirt against her.

The result of this little altercation was a happy compromise, and they went together in the Minister's official car flying the Union Jack. They somehow got to the hotel and found a disabled Russian tank and a few dead soldiers in front of it. The building had suffered a good deal of damage and was being used as a local Russian headquarters. On approaching the door to enter, a Russian sentry brusquely knocked the Minister's Diplomatic Corps Pass out of his hand on to the ground and barred their way. However, a member of the hotel staff who spoke Russian went to their assistance and persuaded an officer to let them in. After a short time they emerged unscathed with a couple of British subjects, and an unexpected bonus in the shape of a Frenchman and German who were enjoying the pleasures of attending a paper manufacturers' conference.

The Freedom Fighters were having some surprising success against the Russian forces, their most effective weapon in the circumstances being the petrol bomb thrown on the louvres of the tanks, and often dropped from the upper windows into the armoured personnel vehicles carrying soldiers. The Russian vehicles had to drive through narrow, old-fashioned streets to reach the centres of resistance and were thus helplessly vulnerable to this form of guerilla attack. The streets in these areas were littered with burnt-out disabled tanks and other vehicles, and the dead bodies of Russian soldiers were lying around in some profusion. The extent of the casualties they were incurring must certainly have been of some considerable concern to the Russian authorities. In the later stages of this first phase of the uprising reports came in of fraternisation between the

Russian forces and the Hungarian people. Certainly Russian tanks were seen going about the city carrying on them Hungarian people and children in almost a carnival spirit. There were reports of a number of incidents when Russian soldiers discussed the situation with the Hungarians, and it seems certain that many of them were sympathetic with the aims of the revolution.

Probably the most deplorable incident of the entire uprising occurred on 25th October when the great massacre took place. Several thousand people had gathered in a large square in front of the Parliament buildings: they were completely unarmed citizens, including large numbers of women and children, in a peaceful demonstration. Suddenly machine-guns opened fire on the crowd; estimates of the number of people killed vary, but it must have been in the region of four to six hundred. Responsibility for the shooting has been placed on both the AVO and the Russians, but most certainly Russian tanks took the larger part. The horror and carnage of the scene appalled the most hardened and callous of imaginations, and the shocking facts of the event need no elaboration—they speak for themselves. No doubt the Communist leaders have placated their consciences with their well-known principle that the end justifies the means. The Military Attaché was walking in that part of the city at the time and witnessed much of the proceedings. It seems that the enormity of the débâcle was quickly realised by the authorities, who rushed lorries to the scene and carted away the bodies by the wagon-load in a non-stop service.

Despite the increasing domination of the situation by the Freedom Fighters at this stage there was always an element of hazard in travelling about the city, particularly after dark. On one evening the *Daily Mail* correspondent, Noel Barber, accompanied by Sefton Delmer of the *Daily Express* and a Hungarian friend, went out in their car against the advice of the British Minister, who warned them of the dangers but, as he commented at the time, journalists, and foreign correspondents in particular, are a law unto themselves. After travelling a short distance a Russian sentry fired on them with a sub-machine gun, shattering the windscreen and splaying the car with bullets. Noel Barber was hit and somehow Sefton Delmer managed to get the car back to the British Legation. Noel Barber was laid, almost unconscious and with blood streaming from his head, on the floor of the office of the Minister's secretary.

Mrs. Fry, who had done her war service in a hospital, swabbed him down, staunched the wound and generally kept him alive until the Hungarian doctor could reach the Legation, a feat he gallantly achieved on a bicycle. He put 40 stitches into Noel's scalp. The problem then arose of how to get Noel to hospital; this was accomplished somewhat hazardously in a Landrover of the British Legation, which itself was fired on during the journey. This incident evoked Leslie Fry to recall the advice of his father who, when on leave from France in the First World War, pointed out that 'dead heroes cannot peel potatoes; do your duty but take no unnecessary risks'.

While all these events were taking place in Pest there was, naturally, no little concern in the Legation about what was happening to the families cut off in Buda, as the bridges remained closed until 28th October. There had been heavy fighting in Buda, some of it in the residential areas and among the houses. The noise of the fighting was in fairly close proximity to some of the houses and was indeed frightening as it swayed around; Russian tanks drove through the streets, and much of this rumpus went on throughout the night. Fresh food ran out and no bread was available; one wife filled the gap by making bread with baking powder, and vowed never to be without yeast again. Most of the telephones remained in operation and Mrs. Fry kept in touch with as many families as possible, offering sanctuary in the Residence to any who were in distress. The first Secretary of the Legation lived a short distance from the Military Attaché; the telephone in his house remained in operation throughout, but the Military Attaché's went out of action early in the proceedings. The wife of the First Secretary, Betty Cope, maintained contact with the Military Attaché's wife and, on one occasion, about midnight, braved the curfew and the black-out to deliver a message warning of evacuation.

By 27th October the fighting had become localised in more determined areas and in general it had diminished to some extent, allowing a greater degree of freedom. It became apparent that night that some movement across the Danube bridges was becoming possible and it was decided to recover the families of the British staff from their beleaguered isolation and to bring them into the Legation. This was done early the following morning, and as they slipped across the river amongst the remnants of Russians and debris all were safely gathered in without incident, bringing their bedding and light fantasies to join the campers in the Legation. No little relief was felt by those already living in their offices, as there would now be someone to do the cooking. Supplies of food were limited to the stocks in the Legation families' shop and no-one knew how long they might have to last. Cooking facilities were only those in the small flat at the top of the Legation, sufficient for about two people. It was a remarkable feat by the wives that they somehow managed to keep every-one fed. Surprise was expressed by one wife who, after having prepared a mousse from a mountain of tins of salmon by hand, found she had lost all her nail varnish. Adding, no doubt, an unexpected relish.

Gradually over the last few days of October a situation akin to stale-mate began to develop in the fighting, and as observers could move more freely the situation became more apparent. It was obvious for all to see that the Soviet troops had suffered incredibly high casualties amongst men, tanks and other armoured vehicles. Burnt-out and disabled tanks and armoured personnel carriers lay about the streets in the areas where the fighting had been heaviest; and the bodies of dead Russian soldiers were scattered in profusion. Clearly it was far more than the Russians had bargained for, and it must have become apparent to them that they could not continue in the *ad hoc* way in which they appeared to have entered the fray. Although fighting was still going on in some parts of the city the Russian forces seemed to have pulled out of the fiercest areas. The Freedom Fighters had not achieved the remarkable results they had without heavy casualties in their own ranks, and many had been buried in hasty graves in the city squares where they were marked by small wooden crosses and, perhaps, a few flowers or other appropriate features. Throughout the city the Hungarian flag, with the Soviet emblem of the hammer and sickle cut out, hung in what seemed a never-ending display in every street. But hanging also amongst them were black flags of mourning, and in some windows were displayed lighted candles of bereavement. The effect, walking along these streets, could not but raise in any person of humanity an extraordinary sense of mixed emotions. The indomitable patriotism and national spirit of these people, touched by the stark reality of the sombre price which had to be paid in an effort to achieve some degree of freedom for that spirit, can surely never have been surpassed in its devotion.

Apart from Imre Nagy, who was already established in the respect and affections of the people, there emerged as a leader and symbol of the Freedom Fighters Colonel Pál Maléter. Early in the uprising he joined the insurgents, moved into the Kilián barracks and organised it into a virtual fortress, to which its old massive stone construction lent itself. Maleter was to play a leading role as events unfolded in the following weeks.

While the Freedom Fighters were gaining the upper hand in Budapest, the insurgents had gained control in the provinces throughout almost the whole country and some had established their own independent radio stations. The Russian troops in these provincial areas seemed to find it prudent to confine themselves to their barracks.

Another remarkable thing was that the electric power system and the greater part of the telephone network within the country continued to function, but after the first few days telephone and cable links leading out of Hungary were cut and public communication with the outside world was severed. However, the Legation in Budapest, like most British Embassies and Legations abroad, had its own radio transmitter and receiver in direct contact with Whitehall, and when the commercial telephone and cable links with outside countries were severed the Legation radio became the only means of communication from within Hungary to the Western powers outside. This placed on Leslie Fry an immense responsibility as the key man in keeping the free countries of the world fully briefed on the course of events in Hungary. As luck would have it, earlier in 1956 the Foreign Office in London had proposed that, as an economy measure, its radio station in Budapest should be closed down, but Leslie Fry had with foresight managed to persuade them to keep it open.

Throughout the whole time the Legation staff were intensely busy. There was a vast amount of information in both the fields of politics and the Armed Forces to sift and evaluate, and to put into logical form. Leslie Fry was frequently at his desk in his office by 5 a.m. and by the same hour of the morning some of the British members of the Legation staff were out assessing developments of the night. The Hungarian translators employed by the Legation coped with a prodigious amount of material, usually working against time, translating Hungarian news broadcasts, newspapers, news-sheets and all odd messages handed into the Legation jotted on all manner of pieces of paper.

On the evening of 28th October Imre Nagy addressed the Hungarian people on the radio and announced that agreement had been reached with the Soviet Government for the withdrawal of Soviet forces from Budapest. He also said that negotiations had been started to settle relations between the Hungarian Peoples' Republic and the Soviet Union with regard to the withdrawal of all Soviet forces stationed in Hungary. Nagy also promised the organisation of a single State police force and that the organs of State Security would be dissolved. In addition to all this he promised that there would be no reprisals against those who took part in the armed fighting, and the old traditional flag of Hungary was to be restored.

On 30th October the Soviet Government in Moscow announced that they would negotiate a withdrawl of their armed forces, not only from Budapest, but from the whole of Hungary. Sir William Hayter, H.M. Ambassador to the U.S.S.R., reported to London, repeating the signal to the Legation in Budapest, that the promise could probably be relied on. To Leslie Fry and his staff in Hungary things looked very different, as they were aware of many reasons why the U.S.S.R. could not evacuate the country.

With these promises in front of them, naturally enough the Hungarian people were jubilant. They thought they had won. Political parties, the Social Democrats, the Workers' Party, and the Peasants' Party began to reform, and law and order was restored in a remarkably short space of time. Workpeople appeared to clear away the debris and rubble, and telegraph poles were reinstated.The country began astonishingly quickly to return to normal and the agricultural workers drove their carts into Budapest and distributed fresh vegetables, fruit and milk, which they gave away to the people and to hospitals.

As the Russian troops began to withdraw from Budapest the emphasis of the fighting changed from an onslaught on the Russians to an all-out hunt for members of the AVO. The Hungarians hated the Russians and fought them with determination and unstinted courage, and were prepared to die in the process but, while they regarded the Russians as an enemy of their country to be ousted by all the means at their disposal, this did not compare with the bitter hatred they had for members of the AVO, against whom their emotions knew no limits of restraint. To the ordinary person in Hungary, men or women who betrayed their fellow countrymen, subjected them to the most ghastly tortures devised by man, and sent thousands of innocent people to the horrors of Soviet labour camps in Siberia were so vile as to be beyond all consideration as human beings. The Freedom Fighters hunted them relentlessly and the AVO men ran like rats to any burrow they could find. When found retribution was instant; they were either torn or beaten to death by the crowd, hanged on the nearest lamp-post or sometimes, mercifully, just shot. The AVO men resorted to a number of subterfuges to avoid being caught. There were reports that some took to the sewers where they were pursued and fighting took place. Another trick made life rather more hazardous for diplomats. All motor cars used by diplomats in Hungary carried special distinguishing number plates, and at this stage it seemed that some of the AVO men tried to escape using cars with these number plates; consequently any bonafide diplomat driving through the city was suspect. The Freedom Fighters had set up numerous road-blocks as one means of trying to trap fleeing AVO men, and often these road-blocks were manned by youths probably about 12 or 14 years of age who were armed with sub-machine guns. To be held up by a professional soldier or mature fighter armed with a tommy-gun is one thing, but to have a 12-year-old point a tommy-gun at one's head while one's papers are examined can be a little more uncomfortable.

The people also used this opportunity of comparative calm to effect a change to the landscape. The Communists had erected on the most prominent buildings, such as church steeples or other tall buildings, large red stars which disfigured the skyline, and by various extraordinary means the people systematically removed these until only one or two of the most impossible were left.

The intractable hard-line Stalinist, Ernö Gerö, had been removed as First Secretary of the Hungarian Communist Party, and Imre Nagy formed a new Government more in keeping with the developments of the time. In this Government Colonel Pál Maléter, the national hero of the Kilián barracks and now promoted to the rank of General was appointed Minister of Defence. In that capacity the Military Attaché was able to arrange an interview with him which took place in the Kilián barracks where Maléter insisted on continuing to base himself. Clearly he was sceptical about the situation and did not trust the Soviet Government's promises.

The reign in power of Mátyás Rákosi as First Secretary of the Hungarian Party had been marked by a ruthless subjugation of the people to his rule; any who stepped out of line by making some mischance remark or who criticised the régime were liable to find themselves in jail without more ado. There were many hundreds incarcerated in this way, and after the heavy fighting the Freedom Fighters broke open these political jails and released the luckless prisoners. Some were able to make their own way, but others who had suffered the full fury or maltreatment of the jails were unable to help themselves and had to be recovered in the most humane way possible. One of the missing British subjects about whom Leslie Fry had continuously been pressing the Hungarian Government for information, only to be assured that they knew nothing about her and that she had left the country, was Dr. Edith Martin, and she walked into the Legation at this time when the political prisons were opened. She was Hungarian by birth and a British subject by marriage who had disappeared over the years. She had spent seven years in solitary confinement in Budapest. She was sent by car immediately to Vienna.

The Legation received innumerable requests from local people for political asylum, some of them in desperation, but all these had to be refused as sympathetically as possible, as it was the policy of H.M. Government not to grant asylum. Only genuine British subjects were allowed sanctuary in the Legation in order that the integrity of its diplomatic immunity should not be violated.

Discussions were held in the Legation about evacuating the wives and families to Vienna, as reports had been received of strong Russian reinforcements entering the country. Despite the excellent work the wives were doing it was decided that it would be better not to have wives with children caught up in a heavy Russian counter-attack, and so a convoy was arranged of the private cars of the Legation staff, mainly driven by the wives, which set off for the frontier early the next morning under the command and guidance of the Air Attaché. The cars were well adorned with Union Jacks, and notices were displayed on the windscreens, written in Russian, denoting the neutrality of the British occupants. There was some apprehension about their getting through; however, they were lucky, and, after driving through several Russian positions on the road, they arrived safely at Nickelsdorf on the Austrian side.

At this phase in the uprising the country began astonishingly quickly to return to normal, but to the staff of the Legation and to many thinking Hungarians there was a horrible ominous atmosphere, despite the euphoria of the people who displayed considerable optimism, misplaced as events proved. After all, they had a Russian promise that the country would be vacated; Imre Nagy had formed a Government, and many moderate leaders, who were of course Communists or certainly Left Wing had come together. Everybody thought that there would shortly be elections and that Hungary would have, at least, a measure of autonomy, if not full independence. This showed a lack of realism, as events proved, but at the time there was little doubt that the people thought they had won. This state of affairs lasted until shortly after midnight on the night of 3rd/4th November, when, to a co-ordinated plan, some 2,500 Russian tanks re-entered the city and Russian artillery began shooting down into Pest from the high ground to the west of the Danube. Then the fighting began again.

The weight of the Russian counter-attack on the city brought an influx of British subjects into the Legation. Word had got around that the building had substantial cellars capable of withstanding a fairly heavy bombardment. Nearly the whole of the British Press correspondents sought sanctuary, although some left to fend for themselves after the first dew days. Being unable to go out because of the intensity of the fighting and curfews, and being unable to send their stories to their papers because of the complete break of international communications, the journalists found themselves in a situation of deprivation to which they were not normally accustomed but, apart from some being a little like caged animals, they bore their frustration with fortitude and gentlemanly sangfroid. Certainly they had to put up with some pretty bare 'hard-lying' conditions as there was no accommodation, and they had to sleep on an odd chair or curl up in the least draughty corner. They were a courageous, cheerful and good-humoured party who lived up to the very best traditions for which British foreign correspondents are renowned. One or two press photographers pursued their craft by taking photographs out of the Legation windows, but quickly found discretion wiser when they became targets for Russian machine-gunners. It was later reported that Russian troops had orders to shoot anyone found taking photographs.

In all there were between 70 and 80 souls in the Legation at this time, and Leslie Fry became anxious about recovering all the expenditure for the staff canteen; even had there been time, it was virtually impossible to keep track of everything each person consumed. He therefore sent a signal to the Foreign Office suggesting that Government, in the somewhat unusual circumstances, should make good any difference between the expenses incurred by the Legation staff and the amount of money which was finally recovered from the guests. Few signals have had so swift an answer. It was to the effect that strict accounts must be kept, and written undertakings to pay all bills later be obtained from those not able to pay cash on the spot. As was to be expected everyone played the game and the staff were not out of pocket.

At times a considerable amount of fighting took place around the Legation, which was not entirely unscathed as broken windows and bullet-marked walls showed. Diplomatic immunity suffered a sharp surprise when a machine-gun bullet whistled through the window of Leslie Fry's office as he sat at his desk, and buried itself in the ceiling above his head. He expressed his indignation in characteristically measured terms, doubtless, with nostalgic memories of his early training as a subaltern in the Gurkha Regiment.

There is no doubt that in this second assault on the city the Russian 'steam-roller' was well at work, and the tanks and artillery used the full weight of their armament to reduce to rubble by heavy bombardment points of resistance in a relentless progress. But still the Freedom Fighters stood their ground, and contested every attack by the Russians by any means they could devise. They only gave up when the building around them was smashed to pieces and in most cases the defenders were dead. If ever there was a fight to the finish this was it, but against what odds and with what desperation?

Throughout the uprising and particularly during this second assault the mass of the Hungarian people were convinced that the Western Powers would go to their aid; they simply could not understand that military help was not forthcoming, and there were constant rumours that Western troops had landed. As the Hungarians saw it, they were fighting a battle for the West against U.S.S.R. Communists and, in those circumstances, the Western Powers were bound to help them. The Legation received many telephone calls from beleaguered strongpoints with nerve-stretching pleas of desperation, some saying they were running out of ammunition and would the Legation send them replenishments. One call was from a defence point saying that Russian tanks had arrived to attack them: shortly, they said, they would be dead, but 'For God's sake do something to save Hungary'. Such calls were sincere cries of dying people, deeply moving to the Legation staff—but neutrality was the rôle that had to be played. At the same time the Legation received an almost constant stream of Hungarians appealing for political asylum, but always the stand had to be made that help could only be given to British subjects.

The importance of the Legation radio link with the outside world has already been stressed, and at this time of the height of the battle it was working at enormous pressure. One evening the radio operator, Jimmy Green, reported to Leslie Fry that he had reached the end of his tether. He had been at his set for two days and two nights with no sleep and could go on no longer, whereupon Leslie Fry took him to his secretary's office, where they split a bottle of champagne to sustain themselves through the arduous times. Jimmy Green was later awarded the M.B.E. in recognition of his services.

Political events after the return of the Russian forces moved quickly if somewhat obscurely. General Pál Maléter and the Chief of Staff of the Hungarian Forces had been arrested by the Soviet K.G.B. when they had been lured to the Russian Headquarters on the pretext of negotiating the withdrawal of Russian Armed Forces from Hungary. The Government of Imre Nagy disintegrated and Nagy and some of his colleagues sought refuge in the Embassy of the Yugoslav Republic. The situation in the country was confused; in some areas the Russians gained control, but in others the Nationalists were still in command, still fighting. There were numerous radio stations broadcasting, some under the control of the Nationalists but others taken over by the Russians. A new Hungarian Government was set up by the Soviet Union called the Hungarian Revolutionary Worker-Peasant Government. This was led as Prime Minister by János Kádár, who had replaced Gerö as First Secretary of the Hungarian Communist party. Earlier in the uprising he had disappeared to Moscow and now returned to head this puppet Government. He officially moved into Budapest in Russian armoured vehicles on 7th November and installed himself in Parliament Buildings. Attempts were then made to bring the country back to normal and to get the workers back to the factories. Nevertheless, despite his appeals, and appeals by some Russian Commanders, fighting and resistance by the Freedom Fighters continued wherever it could.

Despite his claims to represent the people, Kádár was regarded by them as a traitor and was treated with contempt; certainly he had no hope of restoring order and normality on his own, but only by the force of Russian troops, and even then it took him many weeks to obtain the minimum control. It was at this time that the great betrayal of Nagy and his colleagues took place; the Government gave assurances that Nagy and his party would be unmolested and free to leave the Yugoslav Embassy and return home. A bus arrived at the Embassy, ostensibly to take the party to their homes, but instead drove straight to the Russian headquarters where they were all arrested. Two members of the Yugoslav Embassy who had boarded the bus to supervise the safe conduct were ejected roughly by the Russians during the journey. Such was the integrity on which the Hungarian people could place their trust in their Russian brothers.

From time to time friendly demonstrations by Nationalists formed outside the British Legation, singing their national songs and appealing to the Minister for Western aid, and calling on him to convey their grievances to the British Government and the United Nations. In order to counter these demonstrations the Russians sometimes posted tanks outside the Legation on the pretence that it was necessary to protect the Legation from the demonstrators. They were told firmly by the Head of Chancery, 'Kit' Cope, that no protection was necessary and asked to leave, and eventually they gave up their unwelcome attention. During one lunch hour when this was going on, as a form of light relief, some of the British girl secretaries in the Legation amused themselves by teasing the soldiers in the tanks from the upper windows by throwing balls of paper at them. This made the Russians very angry and, of course, the more angry the Russians became the more delighted and persistent were the girls. Finally, one of the Russian tanks, whose commander could obviously restrain himself no longer, drove his tank up to the Legation doorway, thrusting his main gun right inside. If the door had been wide enough he would probably have driven his tank inside as well.

One of the last organised demonstrations was a gathering of some 2,000 women, all dressed in black, in the square outside the Legation. They came together there from all parts of the city in sombre processions or clusters, and they congregated so that the whole seemed to form a funereal cloud. They sang the Hungarian National Anthem and national songs, a great gesture of mourning and despair tinged with the unsuppressable national pride which characterised the whole uprising. The whole episode was the more impressionable by its simplicity, but the pathos and grief it expressed was overwhelming. The Russians lost little time and set about dispersing the gathering by driving their tanks amongst the assembled women, forcing them to scatter for their lives. Some observers regarded this as their most poignant memory and one which they will never forget or recall without the emotion of the moment returning.

The sheer weight of the Russian assault which never faltered, gradually wore down the Hungarian resistance, as it relentlessly eliminated one strongpoint after another, and the fighting continued sporadically until 11th or 12th November. Desperately trying to persuade the Hungarian people to stop fighting, and to restore some normality, Kádár held talks with workers' delegations in an effort to put an end to the strikes which were paralysing industry and made a number of promises. There were to be no reprisals against Freedom Fighers and he pledged to abolish the Secret Police. He undertook to hold new elections and include non-Communist parties in Government. He claimed that Imre Nagy was not under arrest and that he had the choice of participating in Hungarian political life. Kádár must have been aware that, even if he himself had some idea of bringing about these things, his Soviet masters would never allow him to fulfil these promises; however, they helped to persuade the people to lay down their arms.

When it was possible to move about the city again the damage and devastation in many areas was so extensive as to be a wave of tangled destruction. Some streets were impassable, with large blocks of masonry strewn around, tramlines ripped up to form barricades and the overhead wires trailing from their standards. Building after building was reduced to rubble by the Russian bombardment, and clearly the Russian forces had been ruthless in their attacks, simply destroying any building which stood in their path. It was reminiscent of some towns through which heavy fighting had taken place in World War II, and was evidence of the tenacity and desperation with which the Hungarians had fought to obtain some national freedom, and the extreme measures to which the Russians had had to resort to eliminate them.

Although the United Nations had looked the other way and left the Hungarian people to their fate, the International Red Cross had mounted an operation to provide supplies for the hard-pressed people of Budapest, whose stocks of many things were exhausted and who were on the point of starvation. The food supplies were naturally intended as aid to these people, but reports were coming in that it was mainly being distributed to members of the AVO and Party Leaders and their families. One Hungarian woman complained about this to the British Legation as she had been unable to obtain help, and the Commercial Attaché (now Sir James Cable, K.C.M.G.), visited the headquarters of the Red Cross to investigate. The woman concerned was promised help with alacrity, but the disposal of the bulk of the food was still obscure.

As the fighting died down the AVO, with the protection and assistance of the Russian troops, were back in action; mass arrests of hundreds of people were made, mostly indiscriminately. They were summarily sentenced to long terms in Russian labour camps and despatched in train loads to Siberia. Almost certainly many were never to return, even if they survived the rigours for very long. There is no Act of Habeas Corpus in Communist law; it would be inconvenient. So much for the solemn promises of the Soviet Government and of Kádár himself.

Clearly much thought was given in Western circles to the calls for help by the Hungarian people, but Hungary is in a tragic geographical and political situation. On one side is Yugoslavia, a Communist-aligned country, Rumania, a Communist country under Russian control, a stretch of common Russian/Hungarian frontier, then Czechoslovakia, another Russian-ruled country; and finally neutral Austria, whose neutrality is guaranteed by Britain, France, America and the Soviet Union. Consequently no Western intervention could have been carried out without violating somebody's territorial integrity. Leslie Fry recommended and continually pressed for the despatch to Hungary of United Nations observers. These would have been powerless to stop Russian tanks, but their presence might have caused the leaders in the Kremlin to think again about further aggression. These observers would have been on the spot and able to say they were there: 'We were eye-witnesses to the destruction wrought'; 'We watched these events take place'.

However, the course of the turmoil in Hungary was thrown into some confusion by a twist of fate far beyond their control when, on 31st October 1956, French and British forces mounted a campaign on the Suez Canal in an effort to retain their rightful ownership in the face of nationalisation by President Nasser of Egypt. To Western observers in Hungary this was a devastating blow to the Hungarian fight for freedom, which placed so much hope in action by the international community to support its cause in the Security Council and General Assembly of the United Nations. In the British Legation it was apparent, in the face of this turn of events of such world-wide significance, that Suez would over-shadow the affairs of Hungary which, to the United Nations, would from then on be regarded as a triviality. Clearly, the unfortunate Hungarian goose was being irrevocably cooked, and the chances of the Hungarian people in that world forum were virtually 'left at the post'.

An episode which excited the interest was the appearance on the scene of Cardinal Mindszenty, the Roman Catholic Primate of All Hungary. He had been one of Mátyás Rákosi's victims some years before when he had been sentenced to death, but the sentence had been com-muted to life imprisonment. After being held as a prisoner for some eight years he was released by Freedom Fighters on 30th October to be reinstalled. His freedom was short-lived for, as the Russians returned to dispose of the Government of Imre Nagy, Mindszenty made a hazardous escape from the Parliament Buildings to seek refuge in one of the Western Missions. The obvious place for him to make for would have been the Italian Embassy, but that was too far away in the midst of the Russian tank operations then going on, and he managed to reach the American Legation, which was the nearest to Parliament. There he was given political asylum and remained a guest of the Mission for many years.

At the time of the uprising the Indian Government had close relations with the Soviet Union and were not without influence in that sphere of international relations. Leslie Fry, with his long experience of that country, was quick to spot the significance of this situation, and when an Indian diplomatist was in Hungary at the time of the Russian assault he loaned him a collection of then unpublished photographs which had been given to him by a Hungarian. These were clear evidence of the havoc being wrought by the Russian forces, and Leslie Fry thought it important that Pandit Nehru, that non-aligned statesman, should be made fully aware of the realities of the uprising. Leslie Fry also arranged for this visiting diplomatist to interview some ordinary Hungarians, but this turned out to be a worthless and bleak effort as the Indian, after listening to them, told them they could not be telling the truth as their stories did not accord with the official Soviet propaganda hand-out. The Indian remarked that he had been shown no sign by the Hungarian Government of the scenes they had described. Such is the outcome of 'official visits' to Communist countries.

There are times in diplomatic life when the well-oiled machinery of plenipotentorial discourse experiencese frictional moments. Such was one occasion when the Russian forces included in a bombardment a children's hospital, the horror of which provoked the wrath of Mrs. Fry. A blunt Yorkshirewoman, she is probably the only diplomatist's wife to call a leading Communist 'a bloody murderer'. This was at the first meeting after the Revolution and referred to his refusal to respond to Leslie Fry's request to him to intervene with the Russians to prevent further slaughter at that institution. The moment of truth later had a touching and happier ending when, as the Frys were finally leaving Hungary and the usual farewells were being made at the railway station, this man arrived with a large bouquet of flowers for Lady Fry, not of red carnations, which would have been traditional, but white. It will be recalled, of course, that Leslie Fry was awarded a Knighthood in the Order of St. Michael and St. George in recognition of his services during the Hungarian Revolution, and having arrived in Hungary as Mr. and Mrs. L. A. C. Fry, they bade their farewells at the end of their tour as Sir Leslie and Lady Fry.

Leslie Fry and the Legation staff, and indeed all other Foreign Missions, were relieved to see the end of the bloodshed. The Diplomatic Corps was left in a sombre mood and it could only have been a very callous person who failed to share the grief of the Hungarian people in their mourning. This mood was deepened by the omnipresence of the Russian troops, and the knowledge that the AVO were back at their gruesome task exacting retribution on the helpless and innocent simple people.

The British Government was indeed fortunate in having Leslie Fry as its envoy in Budapest at this turbulent time of European history. The combination of his outstanding qualities of military training coupled with his long experience and high ability in the field of diplomacy enabled him to rise to a unique political/military situation in a manner born to such an exacting occasion. His responsibilities were high and he and his Legation staff responded to them with resource, skill and vigour in conditions of difficulty and sometimes even hazard. On a subsequent visit to London Leslie Fry was honoured by his Sovereign with an Audience, and the role of the Legation was acknowledged by its status being upgraded to that of an Embassy.

On a lighter note, Leslie Fry's Netherlands colleague after the uprising was called to The Hague by his Government for consultations and his Sovereign honoured him with an audience as, similarly, Leslie Fry's Sovereign had honoured him. It was related that during the course of it he delicately hinted that a transfer to a rather less exacting post would be welcome. It was not the Revolution that had disturbed him, but it would be a pleasant change to serve in somewhere like Vatican City, free from anxiety that his house and office contained listening-devices. 'But how could you be sure', asked Her Netherlands' Majesty, 'with all those Cardinals about?'

It was at least three months after the uprising had been finally crushed before Leslie Fry and his wife felt disposed to go to any public function or entertainment. The doyenne of the Hungarian musical comedy stage invited them to attend the first night of a revival of 'The Count of Luxembourg' in which she was to appear and was justifiably sure of yet another great success. After all, life had to go on and the people needed a tonic. This star of the show was a national figure who had enormous popularity in the country and was a reigning toast for longer than it would be gallant to recall. She had every attribute of classic blonde beauty, and knew every art and craft of the stage; her personality more than made up for the steadily diminishing amount of dancing she did. While the girls got on with the high-kicking, she moved a few graceful steps from side to side in the centre of the stage. Leslie sent her a bouquet that had been specially made in concentric circles of the national colours of Hungary, red, white and green. Contrary to usual practice, she did not have it brought out to her at the end of the operetta but she carried it on to the stage herself, between the curtains which had fallen after the second Act. The magnificent full evening dress she was wearing set off the colours to perfection and, as one, the audience rose in silence—the dress was black.

Chapter Eight

HUNGARY, 1956

By Group Captain W. D. David, C.B.E., D.F.C., A.F.C., R.A.F. (Ret'd.)

Although more than 20 years have elapsed, it is easy to recall my apprehension prior to that first meeting with Sir Leslie Fry—Her Majesty's Minister (H.M.M.) in Budapest. I was reporting to him in May 1956 upon arrival in Hungary to join his staff as the new British Air Attaché, and the reason for this frame of mind was that my predecessor had been required to vacate the post due to some unfortunate incidents which had come to light—all this resulting in inevitable disruption. It had meant my briefing time for the post being reduced from the normal 18 months to a mere five weeks, and the greatest single handicap being my almost total ignorance of the Hungarian language. From all this, I felt it was possible to receive a cold greeting from my new Foreign Office chief.

In the event, the interview quickly became happy and constructive, for Sir Leslie's welcome to Budapest was warm and sincere. He soon dismissed the language problem and pointed out that one could learn something about it whilst in post. His other advice was to settle in gently and 'to-slowly-take-up-slack'. Having been a soldier in India prior to joining the Indian Civil Service and later transferring to the Foreign Office, he knew much about the role confronting a Service Attaché taking up his first diplomatic post. Sir Leslie was adamant that all entertainment and attendances at official functions should be counted as work—he insisted that it should all be planned as part of the daily task. His words about the Attaché's more interesting rôle—that of touring about the country—were invaluable. He said, with a real twinkle in his eyes, 'I give you a free hand, Dennis, do what you must but never take unnecessary risks'. In those days, conditions were delicate for Attachés when serving behind the Iron Curtain, and it was not unknown for Western Attachés to be forcibly detained by State Security Forces when a Communist régime decided to create an incident. With this in mind, it was agreed that I should always ensure Sir Leslie was informed of my itineriaries in case it became necessary to start enquiries.

My first impression of Sir Leslie was that he was a man whom it would be a pleasure to serve and that he was a fine ambassador for Britain.

This first impression was to be confirmed time and time again during my tour in Hungary.

Most of the summer months of 1956 were taken up with the normal duties of an Attaché—attendances at functions, making contacts, getting to know one's fellow Attachés—East and West—setting up one's own residence, getting to know the staffs of the British and other Missions in Budapest—with particular reference to the Hungarian protocol sections —but much emphasis had to be given to touring about the country, as my post had been unoccupied for several months. This latter activity could be dangerous at times—it is no secret that Service Attachés behind the Iron Curtain had to seek and confirm reports about Soviet and Satellite forces as very little of such information was exchanged between East and West in those days. It was an Attaché's task to undertake this work, which could entail visits near to installations, equipment, aircraft, etc.—whenever possible photographs were taken, as these provide the finest method of confirmation. All of this of course not in accord with the wishes of the Hungarian or Soviet military authorities!!

The spirit Leslie Fry built up in those pre-Uprising days proved to be invaluable, and when things became difficult after 23rd October fortunately this team-work was well established and all concerned had earned each other's trust. The AVO (the Secret Police described by Lieut.-Colonel Noel Cowley in the preceding chapter) were interested in our movements, but they were more concerned about the people we spoke to—in fact any Hungarian who made contact with a Western diplomat was automatically pulled in for questioning. The AVO had installed a camera in front of the British Legation—the lenses were actually fixed in the letter 'O' of the signwritten 'Patyolat' (dry-cleaning shop) which was on the opposite side of the road—in this way the AVO kept a record of all people entering and leaving the Legationl This camera was removed by the AVO when the fighting started in October 1956. The locals knew all about the camera and anyone wanting to see me usually arranged a meeting away from my office or my residence, as both were under AVO surveillance. In the case of the house, some of my staff had to report regularly on me and my family's movements—also my visitors were faithfully reported to the AVO by our staff. Knowing how unpleasant this must have been for these poor people, I always left relatively unimportant notes about the place to make their task a simple one. It was also good discipline for me to ensure that anything of real interest never reached the AVO.

Together with Colonel Noel Cowley monthly tasks were planned. We were in a special position as we were of the equivalent rank of 'counsellor' in the Foreign Office set-up. Sir Leslie's F.O. second-in-command was a First Secretary—thus junior to the Attachés. There were never any complications, as the First Secretary was a wonderful fellow and we were happy to follow his lead whenever Sir Leslie was away. This rank position was observed by some other Missions, however, and that is why we (Noel and I) seemed to meet more foreign dignitaries than would normally be the case. There was never any difficulty as there was always much to do—in the case of the Royal Birthday Party, held at Sir Leslie's residence in June 1956, I had to meet and escort the Soviet Ambassador to H.M.M.

Colonel Cowley and his charming wife, Doreen, were a wonderful help to me and my family, and the way they helped us to settle in during those first few months made life so pleasant when it could well have been a different story. I was saddened when poor Noel was suddenly declared *persona non grata* by the Hungarian régime, and he was given 48 hours to leave the country. It was a great shock to Noel and his family, for the reasons for this were obscure. He left Budapest and I felt a great loss of a valuable fellow attaché and friend. Of course, this move meant that I had to keep an eye on the Military Attaché's office as well as my own. (This state of affairs continued for several weeks after the Uprisings and coincided with a busy period.) Luckily, Noel's assistant was a first-class man who made this double task as easy as possible.

I saw Sir Leslie on most days and his views on the political front were enlightening. He never gave up any chance to try and save the many unfortunate men and women who had worked for the British Legation in the past and who had been arrested on entirely false charges—he would spend a great amount of time trying to help these poor people and their relatives. In all this, Lady Fry's forthright attitude to the prevailing 'Geneva Spirit' was refreshing. I was indebted to them both for the way they helped me during those first months in a diplomatic post.

The summer of 1956 ran into early autumn: outwardly the country and its people were going about their business, but it was possible to detect an uneasy calm. The food riots in Posznan, Poland, sparked off a lot of comment, and strangely this coincided with a very slight lessening of press censorship in the national papers. It was strange to be able to read even a mild form of criticism of the Communist régime in Poland—especially about such a matter as food shortage causing a riot amongst the workers in Poland—such words had not been permitted for over 12 years. There is, too, the fact that firm links do exist between Hungary and Poland—a strong friendship binds the two countries and this has been founded on mutual trust over the years. The Polish General Bem had led the Hungarians against the Hapsburgs in a fight for their independence, and there is a fine statue to this great old Polish warrior set up in Bem Square (Bem Tér) in Budapest. The Hungarians were incensed to read that the Soviet forces in Poland had been called in to suppress forcibly the Polish troubles. In this case, the Soviets only used the minimum amount of force necessary, and the troubles were stopped when more food was produced and prices reduced. It was significant that the Poles were not so harshly treated as the Hungarians were to be later in the year. A main reason for all this was the proximity of Hungary to the west. Hungary's boundaries abut the west and Yugoslavia, whereas Poland is surrounded by satellite states under Soviet control.

Following support given to the Poles by the Hungarians (particularly from the student faction) in news and letters, Polish students came to Budapest to thank formally their fellow Hungarian students. To be able to read such news in the papers was something new for all the younger generation—it was 'heady stuff' for a nation starved of any form of free speech or writings for 12 years—the effects are difficult to understand in countries where such freedom is taken for granted—wherever I went in the country or in the streets of Budapest I heard comment about these articles. It all helped to fan the genuine nationalist spirit.

Another factor was the success of the Polish Party's Central Committee on 19-21 October 1956, when real concessions were gained from Moscow for Poland. The Polish students visiting Budapest at the time were understandably pleased with these concessions and such matters were openly discussed at meetings. Suddenly, larger crowds than usual began to form in the city—full of laughing and cheerful people who were from all walks of life. I asked one crowd member whether he was afraid of the AVO coming to break up the gatherings—he said 'This time there are too many of us for those bullies'. I joined up with one large crowd that moved to the Petőfi statue where all sorts of speeches were made and poems read by Poles and actors. (Petőfi, a great national hero, was a famous Hungarian poet who inspired the country in 1848 with his poem 'Arise, Magyars'—Hungarians always quote Petőfi with great pride and adoration.) After a time I left the Petőfi crowd and joined another around the General Bem statue before going back to the Legation to make a report. I heard later that the Polish students had joined in the cheering, laughter and general speech-making around the Polish General's statue. Once again, the crowds were too big for the AVO to handle, although their agents/informers were in those crowds making notes about ringleaders, etc. The Hungarian Army and Air Force were not trusted by the AVO—with good reason, as events were later to prove, when many of these armed forces joined up with the Freedom Fighters to fight the AVO and the Soviet armed forces to try and regain their country's freedom.

Most of the crowd-forming seemed to take place during the afternoon of 23rd October, and by the evening the sizes of these gatherings had reached immense proportions—more and more people were coming into Budapest from outside the city. At some time, Gerö must have called in the Soviet armed forces to quell the crowds, which had grown too great for his AVO to handle. The Soviet forces were spread all over

Hungary and to organise a force big enough to cope with the magnitude of these crowds would have taken time—there was, too, the need to keep their bases secure from any possible attack when large numbers of troops were moved out of barracks. There was already evidence that crowds were getting out of control in other large towns as in Budapest—all of this would have made the task of the overall Soviet commanders a difficult one. In all there were only about four Divisions of Soviet troops in Hungary on 23rd October and these were spread over large areas. Many of these troops had been in Hungary for years and had grown fond of the Magyar people.

By the evening of 23rd October, the crowds had reached enormous proportions and I joined the largest of these in the Heroes Square area—they were happy and jubilant, for they had just managed to pull down the most hated statue in Hungary. It was a monstrous image of Stalin—the Russian dictator who had inflicted so much misery on Hungary through his most apt pupil, Rákosi. The statue of Joe Stalin had been made from many historic statues of old Hungarian heroes—all of these had been melted down to make 'Joe'. The crowd had a difficult job getting 'Joe' down—initially they had attached ropes to his head and pulled with several lorries; he would not be moved. They then cut through the back of his legs with oxy-acetylene equipment—then and only then did they manage to topple the statue to the ground. The crowd then wanted to drag 'Joe' to the Danube and drown him once and for all time, but this proved to be too difficult a task, so they first set about the job of breaking up the statue into small pieces so that it could never again be put together. I was given a piece of Stalin (which I later sawed in two and gave one half to Sir Leslie and Lady Fry—both pieces are still kept as treasured mementoes of the 23rd October). Eventually, I left the crowd in the Heroes Square and drove past the crowd outside the radio station. Here again, I was amazed at the size of the gathering—the crowds were in a happy mood and were shouting at the radio station staff to tell the world that the people of Hungary were demanding that Gerö be removed, together with the Soviet armed forces in Hungary. Their demands were not met as the AVO managed to install a large guard in the radio station. I spoke to many in these crowds—it was interesting to learn that so many ordinary Hungarians spoke English or French. I was told the people had had enough of repressive régimes which Rákosi and Gerö had forced on the country—all with the backing of Soviet arms. They wanted their freedom, and the last few hours of free speech had made deep impressions on the crowds. I asked many why they had gathered together like this on that day, and the general opinion seemed that they had reached a point of disillusionment with the régime which seemed to heap more and more oppressives on their everyday lives. They felt that life was no longer bearable.

As I drove away from the radio station, I passed a convoy of Hungarian T 34 tanks on their way to it; they were not at action stations and their turrets were open with their commanders waving to the crowds. As I drove past the Houses of Parliament on the lower river road, I passed a large convoy of AVO—they were parked but let me pass by—I noted they all looked scared and apprehensive. For them it must have been quite a shock to realise they could not arrest, kill and torture as had been their unquestioned right for many years.

I was later told that the Hungarian Army tanks reached the radio station and the officer in charge walked up to the building calling on the AVO to give themselves up and to let the people in to tell the world the truth of what was happening in Hungary. The AVO replied by firing into the crowd, killing the tank officer and a 14-year-old girl whose body was shown to the crowds. It was at this moment that the mood of the crowds in Budapest changed: before this incident, they had been happy and laughing; now they became angry and even more determined to rid their country of the Soviet Army—they themselves wanted to deal with Gerö and his hated AVO. Suddenly some rifles and machine-guns were distributed in the crowds—they were handed out from nearby Hungarian Army barracks. Later that night, thousands of factory workers from outlying suburbs came and joined the crowds in the fight for their country's freedom; they obtained more arms and the battles began in earnest. The radio station was a scene of heavy fighting, but severe battles started when the Soviet forces arrived. A main for the Russian tanks was the Hungarian Army Kilián (Maria Theresia) barracks which were so gallantly defended by Colonel Maléter and his men.

News was also reaching Budapest about fighting breaking out in Debrecen, Szolnok and Szeged. As more information was received it was evident that the whole country was joining in this Nationalist Uprising to rid Hungary of a régime which had oppressed the people for over a decade. It was certain that the Soviet Army, with the support of AVO units, was fighting a far more complicated and extensive battle than had been bargained for. Certainly the opposition they were encountering was tough and determined; it was as if the nation was fighting for its life—indeed, it was a nation fighting for its freedom.

Events were difficult to follow in those initial days of the Uprisings. The Nationalist Freedom Fighters were composed of factory workers, tram drivers, miners, and people from all walks of life, and they were supported by men from the Hungarian Army and Air Force: but a great number of young men and women, many still in their early to middle 'teens, seemed to be in the van of much of the fighting so much so that they were affectionately referred to as 'The Young People'. These youngsters fought with incredible bravery and Hungarian 'virtus', and there were cases when young teenagers threw themselves against Russian tanks with a soft drink bottle primed with a detonator and filled with petrol in the hope of causing the tank to catch fire. They succeeded on a few occasions, and more than one new Soviet-type '54' tank was 'cooked-up' (set on fire by burning petrol falling on exhaust) by these home-made Molotov cocktails.

The fighting continued in Budapest for some days; it was fierce at times but I managed to get about the city a little on foot. I was able to photograph some of the fighting, but the dull light made this a difficult task. The fighting was spasmodic but could be dangerous, and I can remember being stuck in a small doorway for some moments while a running battle took place between some AVO and a few Freedom Fighters, all youngsters, who gave me a cheerful wave as they hurried after their prey. I had felt very alone and naked in that doorway a few moments before when bullets were passing by a few feet away, but after that expression of youthful confidence, the world suddenly seemed a better place. Such things were to sustain me in the days that followed. On Thursday, 25th October approximately 600 people were mown down in cold blood by the AVO machine-guns. This took place near the Houses of Parliament, and the AVO were positioned on roofs nearby—the crowd was mainly composed of women and children—and this slaughter was only stopped by a Soviet T54 tank actually opening fire on the murdering AVO. Until this had happened, the AVO were amusing themselves by shooting at people who tried to reach the injured.

The Military Attaché and I went about the city as much as possible in order to get information of the daily situation reports. When the seriousness of the situation was established, Sir Leslie ordered all British staff and their families to come and live at the Legation— luckily, the building was a fairly large one, for not only did we have to feed and sleep the staff and families, but there were many businessmen who had been stranded in Budapest when the fighting started. Added to these numbers, we began to collect a growing number of pressmen, for the Uprisings had become a top news item internationally, and the Legation had the only lines of communication open to the outside world.

Events were soon difficult to follow. Two changes in the government took place: Imre Nagy replaced Andreás Hegedüs as Premier on 24th October, and János Kádár replaced Ernö Gerö on 25th October. Both of these changes caused little comment at first—it seemed just another case of Communist 'musical chairs'—but certainly everyone was pleased to see the back of Gerö. Both Nagy and Kádár had been in government before; Nagy had been Premier in 1953–1955 and had been expelled from the Party in 1955, but was re-admitted in October 1956. Nagy was a symbol of the post-Stalin New Course and was generally considered to be a Nationalist Communist. He had considerable support among the people and gradually became the political leader to be recognised. Colonel (later promoted to General) Maléter (the gallant defender of the Kilián Barracks in Budapest) signified the military leadership, and these two were chosen to lead Hungary by the Freedom Fighters in the National Uprisings in October 1956. Nagy quickly reconvened parliament and started a reform programme which included a reorganisation of the government.

The fighting continued, and the news that H.M.M. had referred the Hungarian case to the United Nations was a great morale-raiser for the Freedom Fighters, some of whom were on duty near the Legation, and these always let me pass—they even offered to escort me, but I declined, as it was important to appear neutral as a diplomat should be; personally, I was sad to see so much optimism being generated, for somehow it seemed out of character for the Soviet Army to allow themselves to be quietened down in this manner. A Hungarian officer told me on 27th October that he thought the Soviet tank crews had run out of ammunition—they had not been re-armed after the main fighting and were having to retain a low profile. The Nationalists had fought hard and given greater resistance than expected: both sides were tired and in time the Soviet tanks withdrew, some flying the new Hungarian National flag—the tri-colour with the hammer and sickle insignia cut out of the middle.

All the fighting which led up to the near-lull period had done incredible damage in the city. Glass was eveywhere, as tank main armament had been used extensively by the Soviets and anti-tank fire by the defending Nationalists in the battle around the barracks where many Soviet tanks were destroyed. Every time one of the large guns was fired, a shower of glass fell into the streets; this, together with the hastily-erected barricades, overturned trams, cars and lorries all made parts of the city look as bad as London had been in the Blitz. Another real hazard was the 'live' tram wires which had broken off from their holders, and were giving off large electric sparks. It all added to the general picture of a battle-scarred city, a rôle which Budapest had filled before.

Then there was a period of relative calm—the Soviet troops had withdrawn from the city and the Nagy government began to get on with the business of running the country: but the Russian troops had only withdrawn to the outskirts of the city, and the tanks occupied the airport. Hundreds were parked along the runways and there were sentries everywhere—hardly the acts of an army supposed to be leaving the country. I also spoke to Hungarian Army servicemen who confirmed that the Soviets were bringing into Hungary great numbers of tanks and thousands more troops; much of this was taking place in Eastern Hungary. I reported this ominous news to H.M.M., who included it in a report to London.

In those days, an inscription was carved on the Petöfi statue—just the plain 'October 23, 1956'. This simple memorial was to mark the place

where Hungarians felt the sacrifice of the young and old who had fought
for their country's freedom should be recorded. However, within a few
days of the new régime taking over later in 1956, this simple reminder
was removed. It is safe to say that the inscription is firmly implanted in
the minds of all freedom-loving Hungarians—they are determined that
those who died should never be forgotten. Certainly the régime had
good cause to remember the date for years to come, and each year all
police and servicemen's leave is cancelled and the Soviet troops in the
country also come to an advanced state of readiness every year on 23rd
October. No doubt, there is still some anxiety when this date arrives
each year.

H.M.M. then decided that I should take a convoy of wives and
children out of Budapest to Vienna—the Legation was too crowded, and
as much of the fighting had died down it was worth trying to get through.
I was keen to get moving as soon as possible—especially with the knowledge that the Russians were massing more and more troops in the
country from the east. There were 39 vehicles in all, and we were on
the road for seven and three-quarter hours, on a run which normally
took two hours. The main hold-ups were the many and various check-
points; there were over 25 in all, some Russian and some AVO—but over
half were Freedom Fighters. It was a worrying time for me as I could
never be certain of the mood of the individual troops. A very frightening
hold-up point was a Russian-type 54 tank which was across the main
Vienna road about 20 miles due west of Budapest—the turret was closed
down, and it traversed its main gun so that it pointed directly at my car.
I stopped, with the whole convoy doing likewise behind me, and stepped
out of my car to hold out the Union Jack which I had attached to a
broomstick and tied to the side of my dear old Standard Vanguard. I
then walked along to the tank, feeling very small and wondering what
to do—it was not possible to knock on any door!!—when luckily I saw
the driver looking at me through his small window and waved my arms.
The turret then opened, and I asked the officer in my poor Hungarian if
we could proceed as we were a convoy of dependents of diplomats in
Budapest. As in all my dealings with the Soviet forces, the young officer
was very correct; he intimated that I was to wait where I was—little did
he know that I only guessed what he was saying in Russian. Then he
spoke into his R/T set and obviously obtained permission for us to move.
He then showed more of himself from the turret, smiled and pointed
to the direction of Vienna—I said 'Nazdrovie'—he saluted and I nodded
and then went back to my car and we gently drove past, faithfully
followed by the 38 vehicles. I had more trouble with the AVO check-
points; they wanted to throw their weight about and were obviously
smarting from their defeat in the country: they seemed to have formed
an AVO 'safe' area about 25 miles from Budapest and were abreast the

Vienna road. They tried to make me turn the convoy back, but I became angry and called for an officer. Eventually a dispirited captain appeared, and I introduced myself as *ezredes* David (Colonel David); this and my diplomatic passport had the desired effect. I also possessed two passes which had been made out by myself and the British Consul the night before at the Legation—we used every official-looking stamp we could find—and with the help of a Russian-speaking visitor we made an impressive-looking clearance chit. I still have this pass which seemed to clear most 'obstacles' away. I also possessed a 'mislaid' pass signed by the Minister of the Interior which allowed me to go about the country. This Ministry of Interior pass had been removed from the AVO headquarters when that building had been taken over by the Freedom Fighters, and it had been given to us as a souvenir—it was signed by the AVO Ministerial Chief, and all we had to do was to fill in my name in Russian in the blank space. It worked! The Nationalists were all very helpful and asked if they could help in any way; they were a mixed bunch, some 60 years old and others only in their early 'teens. All were well armed and seemed to be well acquainted with their weapons. There were many Hungarian Air Force and Army personnel manning these Nationalist Freedom Fighter barriers across the Vienna road.

When we reached Vienna, having crossed the Hungarian frontier at Hegyeshalom, and made my report to H.M. Ambassador, Sir Geoffrey Wallinger. He and all his staff were most helpful, and quickly took over the task of caring for the British families. Before allowing the convoy to split I had checked with the other convoy members that they had somewhere to go in Vienna. It was a real relief to be able to tell the Ambassador a true picture of events in Hungary—he sent an immediate despatch to London and I was promised clerical help the next day to send some reports to my own service chiefs in London. Luckily, the phone from Vienna to London was good and much report content was passed in that manner as well.

We returned to Budapest in four hours, and found the city much as we had left it two days ago. A main difference was the total absence of Soviet Army tanks—these had been withdrawn to Ferihegy airport and Törökbálint. In the following days, I drove about the city as much as possible and ventured into some surrounding areas, and it was while moving to the east that I came into a large Russian build-up. I was not held up, but was left in no doubt that I should return towards Budapest. Upon return I reported the 'outside' conditions to H.M.M. in case he wanted to send any of these facts back to London. Ferihegy airport was very closely guarded by Russian troops—the whole airport seemed to be crammed with tanks, lorries, guns, personnel carriers, etc.—and although it was impossible to get close it was possible to make a rough count of the armoured vehicles. I spoke to many locals during these trips and

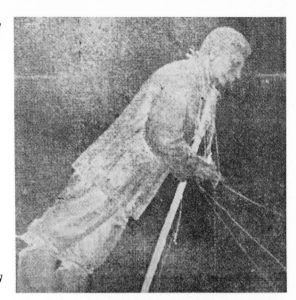

12. (right) *Jo Stalin*
(Associated Press)

13. (below) *Crowd forming up near British Legation*

14. Russian armoured car with crew well forward, under fire

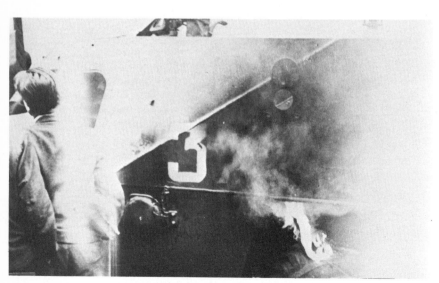

15. Captured Russian armoured car on fire

16. (above) *Captured Russian armoured car, interior*

17. (right) *Hungarian flag with hammer and sickle cut out*

18. *Freedom fighters arriving at British Legation asking for their story to be told*

19. *Upturned tram*

20. Captured Russian tank

21. Captured Russian tank

22. Russian bookshop in Budapest

23. Budapest crowd during a lull in fighting

from one, a soldier who asked me for a lift, I confirmed the fact that the Russians were building up large forces at Vecsés, a town 25 miles east of Budapest. Another trip was made to Tököl airport, normally a Soviet jet bomber base on Csepel Island to the south of Budapest. Now, this bomber base was transformed into a transport aircraft base and many large Soviet troop transports were flying in regularly—more sinister news. One local man told me that over 100 transport aircraft had landed in one day, each aircraft being full of troops. The only two other airfields around Budapest were small and with no concrete runways. These continued to be occupied by the Hungarian Air Force, and there was little activity at these bases, which were too small for any modern jet aircraft to use.

On 3rd November 1956, after obtaining H.M.M.'s permission, I managed to arrange a meeting at the Houses of Parliament with the Nationalist's Chief of Staff—General Kovács of the Hungarian Army—he was a man I had met at several official functions. There was never any question of any political or military discussion during our previous meetings, which had been only concerned with general subjects. I would never have insulted his intelligence by raising controversial subjects, as at all our meetings there was always a political spy in the company. I was amused at one such gathering when a younger and more outspoken Hungarian officer had made a gesture behind the back of another officer in our midst and had then smiled at me—I knew he was pointint out my 'tail' for that evening. For the record, I had already marked the AVO official earlier, he was just too amateurish in his work!

The General was very pleased to see me, and in spite of his being incredibly busy on that day (incidentally, his last as a free man) he gave me a private hearing which lasted for nearly one hour. Initially we had to rely on an interpreter and this caused inevitable delays, but after a while we managed to talk to each other direct. First, I answered his questions and he was glad to have confirmation that the British Legation was sending the truth to the West and that our W/T set was still in action. He was grateful for the stand that Sir Leslie Fry had taken and asked me to convey his thanks to H.M.M. He stressed that Hungary was now governed by the new Nationalist Government, and that its neutrality had been declared. He asked me to pass on a request from the new government to exiled members of the old Horthy régime (pre-Communist era Hungarian government) to keep out of the country—he said that there had been many offers of help from these people. He confirmed that Imre Nagy and the whole of the New Nationalist government were determined to keep a nationalist-type of Communist government. He said that any thought of a return to a Horthy-type government in Hungary was out of the question. Apparently some Russian radio reports had said Horthy supporters were behind the

Uprising, but this was a completely fallacious report and the General was keen the West should be so informed. He confirmed that the behaviour of the old absentee, dilettante landowners in the years before World War Two had laid the foundation for Hungary's eventual Communist takeover. Little or no reforms were carried out on the lands, and the peasants gradually became fed-up with these pleasure seekers. He confirmed that not all were like this, and that many were wonderful people who had tried to improve the conditions for their people and their lands. He was adamant that members of the Horthy party should stay from Hungary as their presence would only cause trouble. He was also keen for the world to know that the Uprisings were brought about by the ordinary people of Hungary who were fighting for their freedom. I asked him exactly what had caused the Uprisings, and said as far as he was concerned there was no organised build-up—it had just evolved, and he, like so many others, had been caught up in the events. He was a loyal and true Hungarian, but he did permit himself to say that he thought all the repression of the Rákosi/Gerö governments had certainly aroused the anger of the ordinary people.

The meeting with the General continued, and I told him about the Russian forces I had seen coming into the Budapest area, and also told him about my journey to and from Vienna two days ago. He made notes and said that his intelligence showed that there were eight and possibly nine Soviet armoured divisions in Hungary at that time. He added that further Soviet infantry units were coming into the country all the time from Russia and surrounding satellite countries, mainly from Russia, because the Soviets were bringing in new troops and new units. He was in no doubt that all this news was ominous and asked me what I thought; I could only speak the truth and said it all worried me. He said that the more optimistic ones in the government thought the Russians were building up their forces to add weight to the forthcoming talks which were due to take place that evening between senior members of the Hungarian government and the Russians. As this was the first I had heard about these talks I asked if I could be told what they were for. The General said he had his doubts about the real reason, but added, 'Our Premier, Imre Nagy, trusts the Russians', and thought there was sincerity in the Russian request for these talks and intended to attend with his senior members of Government—these were to include Imre Nagy, General Maléter (Defence Minister), who was the acknowledged military leader of the Freedom Fighters, and General Kovács. I said the Russians would undoubtedly be smarting from their temporary defeat at the hands of the Nationalists, and furthermore, as these included men and women from all walks of life, this could only make the situation more delicate. The General agreed and then said, 'The Hungarian Army and Air Force are behind Imre Nagy and the whole country is in agreement with the declared

Neutrality'. The General was calm, and he took me to one side before I left his office and quietly added, 'The Budapest newspapers are being enthusiastic about the future, and we have already achieved much, but I am not fooled by this Russian build-up of forces. Please see that the West knows of our plight. If all goes well tonight, then Hungary would want co-operation and help from the West—if not, then please see that the *West send us bandages*'. This was said with quiet dignity, and it was a very moving moment.

As I left the Houses of Parliament, a Russian General and some of his staff arrived and delivered a formal note to Imre Nagy in which reference was made to the size of the Russian forces in Hungary. It also ordered a conference for that evening at 20.00 hrs. to discuss the situation—no reference was made to the earlier arranged talks. Imre Nagy and Generals Maléter and Kovács were to be amongst those present. This formidable behaviour did not pass unnoticed and all Nationalist Forces were placed on a state of advanced readiness. As ordered, the Nationalists kept rendezvous with the Russians. There was no meeting, but General Serov, head of Russia's Secret Police, was there to supervise the arrests of all these gallant men; they were never to be seen in public again and news of their deaths was eventually published.

At 04.00 hrs. on the morning of the 4th November, the Russians came into Budapest from several directions, a main thrust being from Buda, and this time they were leaving nothing to chance. Special shock troops were in the van of the attacks, and Mongol regiments led in much of this early second-wave fighting—these men were devastatingly efficient, and it became obvious that previous defeats were to be avenged. From my house at the top of Gellért Hill in Buda, I could see much of the fighting below me. The Nationalists fought with incredible bravery, outnumbered and outgunned, but still they kept on fighting. I spoke to some of them later in the month, and some told me they had thought Western troops would be coming to help Hungary as they had believed the propaganda given out by Radio Free Europe.

During a lull in the fighting, I managed to get back to the Legation. H.M.M. had sent a couple of Legation cars to bring in the few of us who were away from the building. I reported to Sir Leslie on return and told him my news. He confirmed the Imre Nagy government had been replaced by the Kádár Government. Apparently János Kádár had been ordered to take over the government by the Russians on 4th November, at the time when Nagy and his team were arrested by the KGB party led by General Serov when they went to attend the so-called meetings organised by the Soviets. This news had reached me at my home by radio broadcasts, but latterly the Free Radio had been superseded by more party-type broadcasts.

The British Legation was very crowded and we had a whole host of newsmen in our midst, who were a cheerful bunch of individuals. They were all firm in their resolution to condemn the way the ordinary people in Hungary were being slaughtered; one and all, they found it hard to say even one good word for Communism in this form. Even the *Daily Worker* correspondent, Peter Fryer, eventually could no longer support the creed, and he formally denounced his Communist beliefs—it was a moving moment. The newsmen were a sympathetic lot in the main, and many tried to help in the Legation with the many problems caused by the over-crowding. I became fairly friendly with young Sandy Gall and Ivor Jones of the B.B.C.

By 11 November, most of the fighting had died down and Soviet tanks patrolled the streets regularly; people ignored them pointedly. A major task confronted the population, that of obtaining food, which task was daily becoming more difficult. No trains had run in the area for 19 days, and large supplies of food and medical supplies were stopped from coming into the country from Austria by the Soviet government.

The saddest phase of the Uprisings now began in earnest—AVO arrests, interrogations and torture. Rigged trials, deportations to Russia and the carrying-out of countless death sentences. Exact numbers are not known, but many thousands of Hungarians were removed and their loved ones heard no more about these unfortunates. No amount of enquiries were sufficient to get even an acknowledgement about these 'missing persons'— they just disappeared after arrest by the AVO. Later, trainloads of prisoners were sent off to Russia, and there were many scraps of paper found along the rail tracks with pathetic messages to loved and dear ones. They were just trying to leave their names before being absorbed into nonentity.

All events which took place during my time in Hungary were overshadowed by the Hungarian Uprisings. Throughout that time I was very fortunate to serve such a fine man as Sir Leslie Fry who was my Foreign Office chief—he was always available to give advice and help. Lady Fry was a great support for her husband and she was untiring in the way she watched his well-being. He was under considerable pressure and had many calls on his time, but somehow they seemed to have time for everyone, and they were both to become my close friends.

Chapter Nine

HUNGARY, 1956: 20th ANNIVERSARY B.B.C. INTERVIEW

Conversation between Sir Leslie, who was First Minister, Her Majesty's Legation, Budapest, 1956, and Gavin Scott, reporter for 'The World This Weekend' programme, B.B.C. Radio 4. This conversation was recorded on the day of Sir Leslie's death, 21 October 1976, and a shortened version was broadcast by the B.B.C. on the following Sunday, in connection with the 20th anniversary of the Hungarian Uprising.

Sir Leslie Fry: The news that something of great significance was likely to happen in Hungary broke about the time that Kruschev at the 20th Congress of the Soviet Union Communist Party had denigrated Stalin and expressed the opinion that there were more roads than one to Socialism. Now in Hungary, the intelligentsia, the writers, the authors, the poets, the journalists, have always played a very considerable rôle and they took this up and, naturally, began to write more stimulating articles than they had produced before and there were a good many demands, for example by the students, that there should be more Hungarian identity. In the middle of July, I think the 18th July, Mikoyan visited Hungary and persuaded Mátyás Rákosi, who was the First Secretary of the Hungarian Communist Party, sometimes called Stalin's most apt pupil, that it was time for him to retire; he was an anachronism. There was something like a couple of days' argument, but eventually Rákosi went, and I think that the very first mistake that was made by the Soviet Union was the appointment, in Rákosi's place, of his closest lieutenant—Gerö. Shortly afterwards there was a meeting in the Crimea between the Russian leaders, President Tito and Erno Gerö. This was intended to kiss and make up after the breach with the Soviet Union by Tito and to show that all was now well. The Communist Party of Hungary was invited to send a delegation to Yugoslavia. Well, at much that time, the Poles began to grow restive. In the event they did not revolt in any way, owing, I think, largely to the influence of Cardinal Wyszinski. But in Hungary this debate continued about a separate road to Socialism; and here I would digress to make the point that the Hungarian people are very different from most of those around them. They are Magyars from the Ural mountains with a very long history behind them, a very difficult history of oppression, and they and the Poles have always regarded themselves on the eastern bastions of western civilisation. For example, in 1848, when the Hungarians revolted against the Hapsburgs, they were suppressed by a Russian army, but it is of considerable significance that Polish sympathies lay with the Hungarians, and General Bem—a Polish general—fought on the Hungarian side.

Gavin Scott: Was it your assessment that the population was getting progressively more frustrated in the period immediately preceding the revolution, or was it something that arose very quickly in the few months beforehand?

Sir Leslie Fry: The answer, I am sure is, that it arose remarkably quickly. There had for years, of course, been a sense of deep frustration. Hungary has an agricultural economy and of course Marxism, Leninism, Communism, if you like, demands an industrial proletariat; well, you can hardly have that unless you have some industry, and so Hungary was wrenched away from an agricultural economy to an industrial one, which meant, for instance, the building of Sztalinváros by thousands and thousands of people who were told, virtually overnight, to pack a grip, and report at such and such a railway station to go and help build this new steelworks. There were, of course, other major causes of dissatisfaction, but if your question is intended to imply 'Did you see an armed revolt building up', then I must, in truth, reply no, and I don't think anyone else did. I think the outbreak of hostilities was, in a sense, almost fortuitous. Gerö, who as I mentioned recently had been in Yugoslavia with his delegation, came back a day earlier than he had planned to Budapest, and on 23rd October had made a speech which greatly disappointed the Hungarian people. He said that there must be no loosening of the ties with the Soviet Union and that everyone had better go home and give up these demonstrations. At much the same time, the students, or delegation of students, had gone to the radio station to broadcast their demands. They were refused admittance and, indeed, one was shot by the AVO—the secret police. Crowds naturally gathered there. Two or more Hungarian tanks went through the crowd towards the radio station, a major climbed out of the turret of the tank and he also was shot by the AVO, and these circumstances caused the crowds really to over-run the natural bounds of restraint. They then went to the enormous statue of Stalin and began to topple it from its pedestal.

Gavin Scott: When did you personally first become aware that this was going on?

Sir Leslie Fry: I would say at much the same time at which we're speaking, on 23rd October. My wife and I, quite exceptionally, had been invited to visit a scientific laboratory some short distance outside of Budapest. This was run by a professor who had had his training in England, had married an English woman and at the outbreak of war in 1939 had moved to the Irish Republic. He'd then gone back to Budapest. Well, in 1955/56, as you probably recall, the Geneva spirit was lapping around us, and it seemed to me that one of the gestures we might make to encourage this was the showing of some films of Calder Hall and places of that kind, and it was in return for that, that the professor running this laboratory, obviously with his Government's permission invited us to visit him, and we went out there. We'd been there only a very short time when he was called away to the telephone, he came back and said, 'I'm sorry, I shall 'have to go now; however, my assistant will show you round' Five minutes later the assisant was called away, and it became clear to my wife and me that our room would be more acceptable than our company so we bid adieu to our hosts and returned to Budapest, and we noticed columns of people, sober citizens of all ages and both sexes, walking, some with wreaths in their hands, through the streets, and I thought this must be the funeral of some important figure or some respected colleague at a factory or something of that sort. In fact, these people were converging on the statue of General Bem, the Polish general, who, as I've explained, helped the Hungarian Army in their struggle against the Russians in 1848. We then passed close to the Petöfi Square. Petöfi was one of the 1848 heroes of Hungarian history and the square was full to overflowing. Now this was most unnatural, unheard of in my experience, and I had been in the State by then for a year. You could just *not* congregate in such numbers. It was against the law. So we went to the Legation and I stayed there. By this time, the students had come along with a lot of leaflets setting out their demands. My wife returned to the Residence on the other side of the Danube, and that was the last we saw of one another for a week.

Gavin Scott: What was your reaction to these events?

Sir Leslie Fry: In a word, I think my initial reaction was exhilaration. Clearly we were living at an historical moment in the history of Hungary and I felt a deep sense of privilege to be able to see it.

Gavin Scott: Did you see, in the early stages, any of the fighting between the Soviet troops and any of the Revolutionaries?

Sir Leslie Fry: There was a good deal of fighting round the Legation itself, but most of it, of course, took place further in Pest near the Stalin memorial. The Russian Army, it will be recalled, had two divisions of armour in Hungary before the Revolution broke out and some of those armoured fighting vehicles, tanks and others, were on their way into the city by about ten or eleven o'clock that night. They naturally made for the main centres where they could hold the demonstrators up, but one's job as a diplomat is not to take part in the fighting but to report to one's Government what is going on, and I'm happy to say that we were fortunate enough to receive a great deal of information. Our telephone never went out of action and some of our staff—I'm talking now of the British staff—went quietly out to observe what they could. For example, the Military Attaché witnessed the massacre in the Parliament Square when the AVO men shot down more than 600 Hungarians.

Gavin Scott: Were you surprised at the initial military success of the Revolutionaries?

Sir Leslie Fry: I think yes. They were unarmed and unorganised. They gained weapons from Hungarians in the Hungarian Army who laid down their arms because they were unwilling to fire on their own people, and of course they raided the Secret Police headquarters and obtained arms there. It is true also that the Russians came in to no concerted plan. They were not quite sure where to go and, therefore, a number of tanks found themselves in narrow alleys where, of course, Molotov cocktails could be dropped on them and put them out of action. But frankly, I was surprised that in four or five days the Russians should have felt obliged to retire in order to re-form.

Gavin Scott: What was the atmosphere like after those first successes?

Sir Leslie Fry: The Russians announced in Moscow through *Pravda* on 30th October that they were prepared to negotiate a withdrawal, not merely from Budapest, but from Hungary. Naturally enough the Hungarian people were jubilant. They thought they had won. The Hungarian tricolour appeared at virtually every window throughout the city and, I think, throughout the country, with the centre cut out. The centre, of course, contained the Communist emblem of Hungary. Political parties, the Social Democrats, the Workers' Party, the Peasants' Party began to re-form. Law and order was restored in a remarkable short space of time. Work people appeared to clear away debris and rubble, telegraph poles were reinstated. The country began astonishingly quickly to return to normal, and the agricultural workers drove their carts into Budapest laden with vegetables and fruit which they gave away to the people. That state of affairs lasted until shortly after midnight on the night of 3rd/4th November, when, to a concerted plan, some 2,500 Russian tanks re-entered the city and, of course, Russian artillery began shooting down into Pest from the high ground to the west of the Danube and then the fighting began again.

Gavin Scott: To what extent do you think the Revolutionaries knew that this had to happen? To what extent do you think they believed that what they had achieved in those first days might conceivably be sustained?

Sir Leslie Fry: I think there was a great deal of optimism—misplaced as events proved—but I think there was a great deal of optimism because speeches were being made. After all they had a Russian promise that the country would be vacated. Imre Nagy had formed a Government, a lot of moderate leaders who were, of course, Communists or certainly left wing. They had come together, they had formed a Government, and everybody believed that shortly there would be elections and Hungary would have a measure, at least, of autonomy, if not full independence.

Gavin Scott: There was a degree of unrealism about that, wasn't there?

Sir Leslie Fry: Unrealism, I repeat, as events proved, but at the time there was little doubt in my mind that the Hungarian people thought they had won.

Gavin Scott: From your point of view, when the Russians came back in again, how did you feel about the question of foreign assistance for the Revolution?

Sir Leslie Fry: I felt then as I had felt throughout. It was a question of getting it to Hungary. Even had foreign asistance been available readily and, after all, you don't mobilise divisions of soldiers or fleets of aircraft overnight, how were they physically to get to Hungary? One of the tragedies of Hungary is, of course, geography. You had Tito's Yugoslavia which, after all, is a Communist-dominated country. You had Rumania, another Communist country. You had the common frontier between Hungary and Russia. You had Czechoslovakia, another Communist-dominated country, and you had neutral Austria. This neutrality guaranteed, of course, by Britain, France, the United States, and the Soviet Union. So military forces, in whatever form, simply could not have reached Hungary without violating somebody's territorial integrity. What I felt might have been done and, indeed, what I begged should be done, was the dispatch to Budapest of a delegation of observers from the United Nations. Admittedly they would have been powerless to stop Russian tanks, but I think their presence might have caused the leaders in the Kremlin to think again about further aggression and certainly those observers would have been on the spot and able to say, 'We were there, we saw the destruction wrought, we watched these events take place'.

Gavin Scott: How long did the second phase of the fighting go on for?

Sir Leslie Fry: It went on from the incursion of the Russians into Budapest shortly after midnight on the night of 3rd/4th November until about the 11th or 12th November, and the centres of the heaviest fighting were the workers' areas, particularly Csepel Island. It's an interesting fact that the first of the barricades and the last to be blasted away from them were precisely the two categories of the population whom one would have expected to support a Communist régime—the workers and the students. But, in fact, they were the two most strongly opposed to the Russians. I think the reason for that was not economic, nor yet intellectual; it was in a word—Nationalism. Quite apart from the severe repression of Hungary and Hungarian aspirations over a period of years, to see hostile tanks in your capital city is, I suggest, calculated to set every patriot's hand against the invader, and this is exactly what happened. The fighting continued sporadically until 11th or 12th November.

Gavin Scott: Was it simply in your view overwhelming military force that ended the Revolution?

Sir Leslie Fry: Undoubtedly that was decisive, but Kárdar, who I may say had disappeared during the first part of the Uprising, *had* held talks with workers' delegations in an effort to put a stop to the workers' strike which was paralysing industry. He promised not to take reprisals against Freedom Fighters, and he pledged to abolish the Secret Police. He said he would hold new elections and include non-Communist parties in the Government. He claimed that Imre Nagy was not under arrest and had the choice of participating in Hungarian political life. In other words, a lot of promises were made to the people of Hungary which helped to persuade them to lay down their arms.

Gavin Scott: What was your personal reaction to this? What was your personal reaction when the second phase of the fighting ended as it did?

Sir Leslie Fry: I naturally was glad that the bloodshed should stop. It seemed quite clear that the Hungarian people simply could not hope to win. They fought as bravely as people could be expected to fight in any circumstances, but their chances of victory were nil. My hope was, of course, that some of the promises made to them would be observed and that Hungary would regain, to repeat a phrase I think I've used before, some measure of autonomy, if not complete independence.

Gavin Scott: What is the moment that sticks with you that has the most emotional significance from this period?

Sir Leslie Fry: The manner in which the Hungarian people went, not once, but twice, to meet the invaders was, of course, immensely stimulating. It gave one an impression of great courage. But, for emotion, I think the most emotional instant that I witnessed was the gathering of some 2,000 or more women all dressed in black in the square opposite the British Legation. They came together there from all parts of the city, and they sang their National Anthem and then they were dispersed by Russian tanks. To me, that is quite unforgettable.

Gavin Scott: Of course, to a younger generation, what happened in Hungary is rather overshadowed by the image of what happened in Czechoslovakia in 1968. How do you compare the two events?

Sir Leslie Fry: I think they are very similar in objective. Both countries wanted a larger measure of what I have called autonomy. Dubček wanted to put a face to Communism. Hungary wanted a larger say in her own affairs. The two incidents are, of course, comparable, but whereas in Czechoslovakia there were very few casualties, in Hungary there were over 20,000 killed.

Gorehill
21st October 1976

Chapter Ten

INDONESIA, 1959–1963

'Student demonstrations in the bedroom'

It is wholly characteristic of Leslie Fry that in his notes on this arduous and not always pleasing penultimate posting, as Her Majesty's Ambassador to Djakarta, he left this humorous comment on student demonstrators in his bedroom, in referring to an incident that he would have been the first to acknowledge had serious overtones. The occasion was the aftermath of the Brunei revolt in 1962, and, in protest against Britain's action in suppressing this uprising, over 700 young demonstrators had assembled outside the Ambassadorial residence in the Djakarta suburb of Menteng. Suffering as he was from an attack of amoebic dysentry, Leslie had watched the crowd from his bedroom window, and agreed to receive its leaders . . . in his bedroom. Three students, escorted by armed troops, then came to present him with a statement expressing their support for 'the revolutionaries', whom they said were fighting only for their independence and freedom. With reports coming from Brunei town that the Royal Marine commandos were mopping up the Limbang area of Northern Sarawak and were on the trail of the local rebel leader, Khariel Salieh, Leslie Fry calmly explained that Britain had sent in troops only after receiving an appeal for help from the Sultan. Britain, he further explained, was bound by treaty to safeguard Brunei's security defence, and had no choice but to respond to the appeal.

By this time, Sir Leslie and Lady Fry (as they now were since Her Majesty had honoured Leslie soon after the remarkable events of the Hungarian revolution) had been in Indonesia for more than three years, and had been involved in many facets of British interests in the islands, as well as of the Republic itself. We are fortunately able to build a picture of these years from interviews with Lady Fry, who had already proved herself an active participant in whatever life as the consort of a diplomat might bring! It was as Sir Leslie and Lady Fry that they had assumed their duties here in Djakarta, arriving by sea, on the 5th March 1959.

The city of Djakarta, capital of Indonesia, was given its present name when, in 1945, Indonesia proclaimed its independence. The original text of the proclamation that ended centuries of Dutch colonial rule (interrupted and forever dispelled by the Japanese occupation of the islands during World War II) was in the actual handwriting of a man whose name has given the international media many a good story to tell, and whose rôle in the development of a new, co-ordinated identity for Indonesia is acknowledged by his opponents as well as by his admirers . . . Achmad Sukarno, the Commander-in-Chief and first President of the new Republic.

The most important aspect for posterity of Leslie Fry's term of office as Ambassador to Djakarta is without doubt the fact that he became personally acquainted with this controversial figure, so far as such acquaintanceship was possible within the inhibitions of protocal and the complexities of Sukarno's own life-style. And we are particularly fortunate in having a first-hand account of Sukarno, written by Leslie Fry himself as a basis for the chapter he had planned on Indonesia in his uncompleted autobiography. He wrote:

'Achmad Sukarno was the sole arbiter throughout the four years my wife and I spent in Indonesia of all official business of any consequence: foreign and economic affairs, public works, general education, and religious instruction—everything had to be referred to him. In matters aesthetic also his judgment was eagerly sought and ecstatically received by the sycophants who attended him. It reminded one of that line in a song of Bunthorne's in "Patience": "And hi-diddle-diddle will rank as an idyll if I pronounce it chaste".

Not that there was anything chaste about Sukarno himself. His sexual appetite was legendary, though how much of the legend was fact and how much fiction it was impossible to say. So far from attracting criticism, however, tales of his prowess were recounted with admiring envy by his countrymen, while in general the women appeared to accept his way of life as part of the natural order of things. After all, the Minister for Religious Affairs until he was gaoled in 1962 for corruption, though goodness knows how he found time for it, had four wives and 28 children. (The fact that it suited President Sukarno to make a scapegoat of the Minister did not go unnoticed. Especially as the matter for which he contrived to have him gaoled was a currency offence involving investment of a small sum in Singapore.) It was typical of Sukarno that a Minister of Religious Affairs, of all departments, was made a butt in this way. The sole criticism I heard voiced was that, as Head of a modern state, Sukarno should have restricted himself to only one offical wife. The operative word is, of course, "official".

Born in 1901, Sukarno (or Soekarno, as the name is often spelt: the "u" and "oe" are interchangeable) was the son of an East Javanese Muslim schoolmaster and a Balinese Hindu mother, of whom he spoke with much affection. This odd inter-marriage would be most unlikely to occur in India or Pakistan, for example, and for that matter was highly unusual in Indonesia—even though Indonesian attitudes to religious differences are relatively more relaxed. It must have contributed a good deal, however, to Sukarno's understanding of the diverse peoples of his country—one of his outstanding qualities.

He also had Dutch blood in his veins. This assertion was made to me by a Foreign Minister of the Netherlands. I had not heard it in Indonesia, but can readily believe it. Sukarno was more physically robust and active than most Indonesians, more thrusting by nature and more obviously disposed to assume the rôle of leader.

We had one physical attribute at least in common. One humid night at a party in the Palace nothing would satisfy him but that we should take our shoes off and stand back to back. As he had noticed, we were exactly the same height.

Sukarno was in effect an old-style Asian potentate with a veneer of modern European attributes, always an actor jealous of his leading part and confident that he could hold the stage against all comers. He had a great talent for devising political slogans and theorising about ideologies, but little for administration and the day-to-day processes of government. As for financial and economic problems, he could not be bothered with them. Foreign aid would surely flow in while the Russians and Americans were there to be played off against each other; and Japanese war reparations would pay for grandiose, prestige building schemes. Meanwhile, Indonesia's economy, potentially so rich, went untended.

Sukarno nevertheless offered the disparate peoples of Indonesia an invaluable service. The only unity they had known was that of living together under Dutch rule. After he and Dr. Hatta, urged on by the revolver-tapping (or so he told me) of Chairul Saleh, the students' leader, had drafted the proclamation of independence—in the British house which is still the residence of H.M. Ambassador—and promulgated it the next day (17th August, 1945), it was Sukarno who seemed to embody national aspirations and who developed a new sense of unity by travelling from place to place, island to island, speaking to as many audiences as could be gathered together to hear him. "Sukarno, Spokesman of the People" was, he told me, the only epitaph he wanted.'

It is evident from the level of exchange between Sukarno and Sir Leslie Fry that the two men had some rapport, and they certainly got on well even within the realms of confrontation that did develop between them. This may have been partly because Sukarno had a genuine admiration for Britain, and also partly because Leslie had served with such success with Pandit Nehru—a statesman Sukarno liked to compare himself with, however unlikely the comparison may seem to the observer.

It certainly implies that Leslie enjoyed a degree of privilege with Sukarno, able to treat him as man to man, when we learn that Leslie produced for the President the unique experience of being interrupted in one of his many public speeches. Sukarno was speaking of the two

Dutch police actions by means of which the Netherlands had attempted to regain possession of Indonesia, and contrasted them with the British transfer of power in India. Pandit Nehru, he said, had gone to see Sir Winston Churchill after India had become independent and had explained India's new aspirations. With a passable attempt at imitating Sir Winston's own gruff tones, Sukarno began to quote the reply—but faltered. He waved an explicit hand. It was obvious he could not remember the phrase. And Leslie, unable to bear it, got up from his seat (on the same platform) and approached Sukarno at the microphone. 'Mr. President', he said, 'the quotation you have in mind is—' but Sukarno interrupted Leslie in his own turn, and invited him to take over the microphone and finish the quotation.

'I have not become the King's First Minister', Leslie repeated on behalf of Sir Winston himself, 'in order to preside over the liquidation of the British Empire'.

It was perhaps greatly to the advantage of the British in Indonesia that Leslie Fry was able to communicate with Sukarno in this vein, and the major activity of his four years there—the organisation of the long-awaited, much-needed new Chancery in Djakarta—depended on his ability to take the initiative, and more, to push the vast undertaking to completion. It is significant that when Leslie was in the audience for one of Sukarno's endless discourses (this time he was addressing University undergraduates, in his favourite rôle of Professor) and the theme was scientific development over the ages, he began to praise British achievement, naming a list of scientists one by one, and culminating in inviting Leslie to stand and receive the applause due to Britain in this field. The respect implied in this gesture for the British way of doing things and the standards of our achievement must have coloured the way in which Leslie was able to apply a free hand in getting the Chancery built. There were minor arguments in the course of the construction, and a running source of friction laced with humour between the President and H.M.'s Ambassador seems to have been the height of the new building, and a misunderstanding based on the European concept of the 'five-storeyed' construction and the British habit of starting to count the number of floors *after* the ground-floor itself.

The site of the proposed new Chancery was on Djalan Thamrin, the planned 'millionaires' row' of the new-look Djakarta which the City Council was developing. Opposite the site was that of the great new hotel *Indonesia*, which Sukarno himself was determined would be completed and in use for the approaching Asian Games. In fact when Sir Leslie Fry arrived in Djakarta he inherited a vacant plot which the Government of Indonesia had granted the British some 14 years previously.

This was all to the good. After Leslie's arrival in Djakarta the first telegram he had sent, as a matter of course, was to say that he had arrived and assumed charge. The second telegram, hot on the heels of the first, ran: 'Never in all my 35 years of Crown Service have I seen the British abroad so meanly accomodated'.

As it happened, Sir Edward Muir, Minister for Public Works, was at that time making arrangements for a tour of South East Asia, with Djakarta *not* on his itinerary! But at the end of the Frys' first month there he did fly out from Hong Kong and spent a night at the Embassy. Leslie then obtained the permission of the American Ambassador, Howard P. Jones, to bring Sir Edward to the magnificent building that housed the American Chancery. There a reception committee was well schooled, and welcoming Sir Edward with open arms Howard P. Jones gave a heartfelt speech about the plight of his British colleagues. As Leslie and Sir Edward paced the tarmac hours later at Kebajoran airport, Sir Edward turned to H.M. Ambassador and said: 'I promise you I will build a new Chancery every bit as good as the Americans'.'

In his book *Foreign Body in the Eye*, Sir Charles Mott-Radclyffe, a Conservative M.P. who had come out to Djakarta as leader of a study group during Sir Leslie's term of service, writes that Sir Leslie and Lady Fry had done a first-class job. Leslie, he describes, as 'bullying' the Ministry of Works into at last building the new Chancery! The unheard-of contemporary luxuries of air-conditioning in every one of the 79 rooms, proper refrigeration facilities, and a private swimming-pool which all members of staff were invited to use, all made a tremendous difference to staff morale. In a posting notorious for high sickness rate Leslie also obtained a resident doctor—a great help to those families with young children. When the building had seemed slow, and it looked as if they were to complete indefinitely for the favours of the workmen who were also engaged on the hotel *Indonesia*, Leslie took the initiative and rented a house for imported Chinese workers, supplying them even with their own Chinese cook.

It is ironical that the will and energy put into this project, the impressive ceremony of the laying of the foundation stone on December 1st 1960 (Plate No. 27) by Lady Fry in the presence of almost the entire British community in Djakarta, and the subsequent brief enjoyment of the whole achievement, should end in a classic sacking of the Chancery by student protestors and vandals—when Leslie Fry had himself shown such courtesy to those earlier 'student demonstrators in the bedroom'. And it is typical of Leslie Fry, when he heard the news (by then he was in Brazil) of the sacking, that he wrote to the then Ambassador in Djakarta, Andy Gilchrist, asking him to take more care of H.M.'s property!

Among the British members of the Foreign Service and others who came and went during Leslie's own term were the Counsellor Ralph Selby and his wife Julianna, who are also mentioned in Sir Charles

Mott-Radclyffe's book, and Miles Ponsonby, who was later to become Ambassador to Ulan Bator. Another interesting figure of this epoch is Dr. Grace Thornton, the scholar, who was to create a controversy all her own when she was appointed Consul in Djakarta—an unprecedented example of non-discrimination against the sexes, and a most futuristic gesture on the part of the Foreign Office itself!

In Djakarta at this time also featured a very active British Council, and the fact that the Indonesians are extremely keen linguists (and English they found a desirable language both in cultural and technical studies) meant that the language classes at their headquarters were always very well attended. This no doubt formed a valuable backing to Indonesia's expanding educational services, and in addressing a first-ever Vacation Course for teachers of English in Indonesia (at Bandung), Leslie noted that it was planned by the Ministry of Education in conjunction with the British Council to provide actual teachers of English in the Indonesian schools—to Leslie the most important, first-base for learning a language—with further training and the opportunities for shared discussion. Leslie had not forgotten how impressed he had been when the President himself spoke to him, after the presentation of his credentials on his arrival in Indonesia, in good English.

The students who packed out the classes organised by Mr. Lawrence at the British Council, however, were not the only members of the Djakarta community seeking to improve their English. And to meet the request of the Prime Minister's wife, Mrs. Djuanda, for lessons for the many ladies who were not necessarily learning the language for reasons of a career, Lady Fry herself—no stranger to running a school since her first days in Budapest—organised classes which were an outstanding success and earned the British community many long-lasting friends. Four English circles were organised altogether: one for 14 Ministers' wives, one for almost 30 Naval wives, another for the wives of engineers amounting to 20, and a similar-sized group for 'Gedung Wanita'—housewives. The classes met every fortnight, and extra coaching was available to those who desired it. Visits to the British Council library were a great treat, and variety was introduced by means of audio-visual aids, such as films on the subjects of 'A Journey on a London Bus', and the Trooping of the Colour, while talks from visiting Britons also contributed variety and interest.

The enthusiasm shown for these classes was quite typical of the Indonesian woman. She has always been socially active, interested in education, and fairly liberated by Asian standards (Indonesian women were the first in Asia to have their own personal bank accounts), and receives encouragement rather than the opposite from her husband or male colleagues. Great strides were made in the Frys' term of office, Lady Fry herself noticed with interest, in the provision of play groups

24. Indonesia: Presentation of Credentials at the Presidential Palace, 18 March 1959

25. Indonesia: Bogor Palace, the country residence of the late President Sukarno. Sir Leslie Fry dancing with a Balinese lady

26. *Indonesia: 'Teachers of English' seminar, 1961, organised by the British Ministry of Education in conjunction with the British Council, Djakarta*

27. *Indonesia: the new embassy, Djakarta. The foundation stone was laid by Lady Fry on 1 December 1960*

28. Brazil: the British Residence, Rio de Janeiro, the front entrance

29. Brazil: the British Residence, Rio de Janeiro, the yellow salon

30. (above) *Brazil: Sir Leslie Fry* (right) *with H.E. Abdol Husain Hamzavi, Ambassador of Iran* (left), *and Dr. Fragoso, secretary-general in the Ministry of Foreign Affairs, Rio de Janeiro*

31. (left) *Brazil: Lady Fry receiving the Brazilian Red Cross decoration from the Acting President of the Brazilian Red Cross, Minister Dr. Alvaro Dias, shortly before the Fry's departure from Brazil on 3 August 1966*

and kindergarten, and the Indonesian women seemed to her well-versed in public and social issues.

The goodwill towards Britain at this time, however the more serious political confrontations might imply to the contrary, were noted also in the broadcasts which Sir Leslie gave annually—at the invitation of Radio Indonesia—on the occasion of the Queen's Birthday. He pointed out that Britain was extending per capita more aid to newly-developing countries than other major powers, and that this he knew to be vital to Indonesia's use of aid from outside. But he found trade more important than aid, and was proud to recall that the first contract to be signed within Indonesia's Eight Year Development Plan for textile mills and their machinery was to be supplied by United Kingdom firms. He was also pleased to record the 10th anniversary of the Colombo Plan, an Anglo-Indonesian development pact, during his term of office.

As part of the fostering of goodwill necessary to his bid for outside aid (from whatever source), Achmad Sukarno made a habit of escorting in person groups of official, or commercial, parties on his own frequent journeys among the islands of Indonesia. Sir Leslie himself was greatly restricted by the work he had undertaken on the new Chancery building, but was able to attend official visits for Heads of Mission of Jogjakarta and to the important region of West Irian. Over the years, within the itineraries Sukarno planned to give not only accredited diplomats but the ordinary visitor to Indonesia a wide view and understanding of the country, Sir Leslie also managed to visit Borneo, Jogja, Solo, and Boro-budor. And of course he visited Bali with great interest: an oasis of Hinduism which had come to Indonesia over 2,000 years before with the Indian traders. Its long volcanic chain—an extension of the backbone of Java—is also typical of the whole Indonesian scene, and the numerous pleasant hotels and the refreshing sea breezes made this a favourite spot. Sir Leslie was also a guest (with Lady Fry) of British Petroleum at Kalimantan, on the occasion of the laying of new pipelines. Otherwise travel also included frequent visits to Sumatra, where Britain had a Consul.

It is no secret that the posting to Indonesia was a tough assignment, marred for the Ambassador by lack of staff, by a difficult climate, bad housing, and a country not celebrated for its good bill of health. After four years in the problematic, tense atmosphere of Budapest, Leslie had frankly hoped for a better posting. He had after all stayed on in Hungary two years longer than normally would have been expected under a Communist regime, and when he had been asked to do so had not demurred. Now he once more found himself on a four-year posting. And his disappointment when he had first learnt that he was to be asked to go to Djkarta is characteristically masked by the fact that he had on principle—the principle learned as a soldier—never turned down an order.

It is to his credit that he made a remarkably good job of a remarkably difficult time, and in fact turned it to good purpose, both as an exercise in representing his country, and as a lasting, authentic record of an historic time, place, and man in the era that was Sukarno's Republic. *The Times'* obituary for Sukarno, who died in June 1970 at the age of 69, in many ways echoed much of what Leslie Fry observed and understood of this charismatic man. It is interesting to speculate how Leslie himself would have featured in the action had his term of office in Djkarta extended to the military risings of 1965, to Sukarno's flirting with Communism—and with the philosophies of Mao. When he surrendered finally to those who bid for power against him, and in particular to General Suharto, early in 1967, Sukarno had given them a good run for their money, and for most of his years as President his particular magic had undoubtedly held him in genuine sway over his people. It is thanks to Leslie Fry that we have some lasting glimpse of the moments when the magic was also human.

Chapter Eleven

BRAZIL: LAST POSTING

By R. J. D. Evans

Leslie Fry arrived in Rio de Janeiro in July 1963. Having reached the age of 55 he had reasons to expect that it would be his last overseas appointment, but also to anticipate that he would serve there for at least four if not five years, before retirement. Settling down in what was regarded as the finest of Britain's ambassadorial residences in the Americas, a splendid British-designed mansion built from some of the blocked sterling balances of the war years, it impressed itself on its new occupant as reminiscent of the fine buildings that in the past had housed the rulers of the Indian Empire in the days of the Raj and colonial governors in bygone times.

But as ambassador to Latin America's largest republic, whose territorial dimensions exceeded those of the United States (excluding Alaska), he was enough of a realist to recognise that his primary task was to foster Anglo-Brazilian trade, and to reverse the long post-war decline in Britain's commercial stake in what the Foreign Office, though too few British industrialists and investors, looked upon as one of the more important of the emergent nations of the developing world.

It was in several respects a daunting task. Some of his predecessors had embarked on it with disappointing results. Something always happened to create obstacles: downward trends in the world economy, instability in Latin America which discouraged British investors from persisting in their efforts anywhere in the sub-continent, or the absence of dynamism in Britain's own efforts to recapture its share of overseas markets and to take advantage of investment opportunities.

But there were valuable assets in Britain's favour which Leslie Fry was quick to identify. Much residual goodwill remained from the days when Britain was Brazil's major trading partner and the country that built its railways, public utilities and communications systems, while simultaneously refurnishing the capital and technologies to enable the enterprising Brazilians to expand on the infrastructure contributed by the British in earlier days.

There was also the enduring respect for England's political institutions. This had been consolidated by her war-time performance, which every literate Brazilian associated with the leadership of Winston Churchill, whose funeral shortly before the arrival of the Frys made a deep impact on the people who had been allies in the concluding year of the war in Europe.

There was therefore a complex of legends surrounding the prestige of the British, linked with the Monarchy, the Mother of Parliaments, Scotland Yard, the Royal Navy, the R.A.F., and the Fifth Army, as well as the earlier experiences when British skills, enterprise and money first helped to embark the Brazilians on the giant venture of 'occupying' their vast interior.

But some of the marks of Britain's past impact on Brazil were wasting assets by the time of Leslie Fry's arrival. Although still operational after half a century, the old iron bridges made in England and shipped in sections across the Atlantic to carry roads and railways into the hinterlands were little more than engineering curiosities for the new generation of Brazilian technologists. The famous floating dock serving the Amazonian port of Manaus, and hinged to serve ocean-going vessels in the wet and dry seasons when the river rose and fell more than 30 feet, remained an object of admiration, while testifying to Britain's absence from the new industries of the resurgent city and free port 1,000 miles up-river.

The British community were sadly shrunk and hard put to maintain the schools, hospitals, cemeteries and social clubs built to serve their needs in the past. And among the new ambassador's responsibilities was that of deciding what to do about them, and whether to advise restoration and continued maintenance, or their final disposal together with the remnants of the former British-owned utilities already transferred to Braailian state ownership.

But not all the trends were negative, and Leslie Fry was optimistic about the opportunities for a British re-entry in line with Foreign Office official directives for Latin America, and especially Brazil. One avenue he hoped to pursue was to take advantage of the great success of the English-teaching centres based on the Cultura Inglesa schools sponsored by the British Council.

With 15,000 young Brazilians attending these courses in several cities, and with requests pouring in for the creation of new centres in others, he became a strong supporter of what had become the largest English-teaching operation in any foreign country. Knowledge of the language, he firmly believed, could provide the kind of re-entry card that British technology and capital had provided in the late 19th and early 20th centuries.

It was with this objective in mind that he became an enthusiastic advocate of the Casa Britanica project for the construction in down-town Rio, on a site being cleared by the removal of the Santo Antonio hill, in which Britain's presence could be concentrated and dignified. His idea was that the offices of the Embassy, the British Council, the B.B.C., the British Chamber of Commerce, and some of the business houses could be better housed and more conveniently located than in the shabby, scattered and old-fashioned premises they were then occupying.

This was all the more necessary, in his opinion, because the embassy proper would shortly be transferred to the new federal capital of Brasilia: it was his hope that the proposed British Centre would help to fill the resulting vacuum in the old capital of Rio which would clearly remain the country's financial and cultural centre.

It was in his time also that the first plans were drawn up for the new embassy building in Brasilia. An imaginative design was prepared by British architects who visited Brazil for the purpose. He regarded the two projects as linked with one another, and forming jointly something of a foundation stone on which to build Britain's new stake, in what was already being seen as an 'emergent power' in the hemisphere.

But none of this was to be. Even if Leslie Fry's tenure of the embassy had been prolonged to a third term, as he had hoped, the prospects for a vigorous British participation in the Brazilian 'economic miracle' of the early 1970s would not have materialised. Ten years after his departure there is no new embassy building in Brasilia, where the staff still works in makeshift premises. The proposed Casa Britanica never progressed beyond his personal vision; and the consulate-general still operates from the obsolete offices in the Praia do Flemengo, which had housed the old Chancery.

Events, already discernible at the time of his arrival, conspired to frustrate the ambassador's sanguine expectations. Brazil was about to enter its time of troubles. After this was over Britain was destined to fall into a period of industrial decline, which was to defer its participation in Brazil's speedy recovery and phenomenal expansion.

Nevertheless, Leslie Fry took up his duties with enthusiasm and faith in the future of both countries, despite some unfavourable omens like the rising political temperature foreshadowing the crisis to come in Brazil, and the evidence that Britain was not holding its own in the Brazilian market.

In 1964 British exports to Brazil were down to £12 million, the lowest for nine years. The following year they were only £10½ million, at which level they sorely tried the ambassador's confidence. Even so, he made a brave attempt to reasure the British business community. Addressing the British Chamber of Commerce in Sao Paulo in April 1966, when Brazil's own recovery was already on the way, he found excuses for Britain's poor performance in 'her very big Defence responsibilities in various parts of the world, aid obligations to Commonwealth countries and other demands on the nation's resources'.

Pinning his hopes on confidence that the British re-entry was only deferred, he tried to reassure his listeners, and doubtless himself by stressing that British technological excellence in the field of nuclear energy, aeroautics and other industries would eventually attract Brazilian buyers. These, he added, 'are among the reasons why I am not too depressed about our current showing'.

It was on this occasion that he broke the news about his own impending departure, and early retirement on reaching the 'notional' age of 60, calculated, as he explained, on the years he had served in unhealthy climates and hardship posts. And it was an understatement when he added that he and his wife would be leaving Brazil 'with deep regret'.

If Leslie Fry was about to leave Brazil a disappointed man, his closest friends knew that this was not so much because of the three frustrated years or any self-regarding motives and a desire to cling to office. The true reason was that he had acquired a liking for Brazil and its people, and sincerely believed that he had a positive contribution to make to Anglo-Brazilian relations.

The idea that he was an Englishman who did not mingle easily with foreigners, and that his formative years in India of the Raj made him unsympathetic to Latin Americans, was a mistaken one. Brazilians, especially, are exceptionally sensitive to how foreigners react to themselves and their country. When they got to know him they soon detected the sincerity of his sentiments, and realised that they were not motivated by professional diplomatic tact used to disguise an innate sense of Anglo-Saxon superiority and an undeclared critical attitude towards their shortcomings.

Some distinguished Brazilian visitors to Britain showed none of their customary hesitation in accepting invitations to visit the Frys in their retirement. They knew they would be made welcome at their beautiful home near Petworth, whether they were leading figures visiting Britain or impecunious students doing post-graduate studies in London.

This was manifested also when President Castelo Branco became the first Brazilian head of state to accept an invitation to dinner at the British Embassy during Leslie Fry's second and last term. As the guest of honour at a banquet for 104 people it was a splendid occasion in a worthy setting. Moreover, it confirmed a temperamental affinity between the former Ghurka officer and the austere general from the State of Ceara in the remote and arid North-East, who braved international obloquy by his assumption (with deep reluctance as was well known to his close associates) of responsibility for saving his country from populism and anarchy by overthrowing a constitutional government and imposing direct military rule.

With his background and experience Leslie Fry was well placed to distinguish between what has to be regarded in fairness as more a necessary surgical operation in the political sphere than a rebellion by power-hungry generals in pursuit of their personal ambitions. Nor was he unaware from his early years in India of the difficulties of ruling a large and turbulent country. His early judgement on the 1964 revolution headed by General Castelo Branco was to be vindicated when the latter lifted the draconian measures imposed to deal with the emergency at the end of six months and when, after completing his two years as President, he stepped down to make way for his successor on whom he bequeathed a draft constitution which would return Brazil to civil rule.

The fact that later events were to frustrate such a return, namely another attempt by the extreme left to recapture power in 1968 after the emergency restrictions had been rescinded, and the outbreak of political terrorism of 1969–1972—the world's first experience of this unpleasant phenomenon—cannot in retrospect be viewed as reversing the judgement made of them at the time by a new but percipient ambassador, who interpreted them as a development which halted the Communist penetration of Brazil, and, through Brazil, of the remainder of the sub-continent to alter the balance of power in the Americas.

The secondary effect of the events of March 1975 was to embark Brazil some four years later on a decade of remarkable expansion, to confirm that the forces at work in the country in the second half of the 20th century were not those of social and political revolution, but of dynamic economic growth. Leslie Fry was not present to witness this development, but he did detect signs that it was this and not the way of Cuba that was to be Brazil's destiny. His first favourable impressions of the country were not altered by subsequent developments, and his valedictory despatch in 1966 did not differ materially from that in which he conveyed to the Foreign Office his 'First Impressions' three years earlier.

A Different Kind of Revolution

Coming after the 1947 massacres in India, the Hungarian Uprising of 1956 and the sanguinary upheaval in Indonesia, all of which he had witnessed from a front-seat position, the Brazilian revolution of 1964 was for Leslie Fry personally a comparatively tame affair. Although in historical perspective it was in some respects the most significant development in the country's history since the fall of the Empire and the birth of the Republic in 1889, which led to the transfer of power from the old slave-owning, sugar-growing plantation oligarchy of the North-East to the coffee-growing barons of the Centre South employing free immigrant workers from Europe, it was bloodless and brief.

Yet it was enormously significant. This time the consequence was not so much a transfer of political authority from one region to another, or from one vested economic group to a successor, but, as it were, the diffusion of power and influence more widely from what had been traditionally successive centres of gravity created by cyclical changes originating in world trade, to engage the nation as a whole.

Moreover, the forces at work were internal. They were not engendered, as in the past, by the impact of international trade on a primary-producing and export-orientated economy, so much as by the growth of the domestic market and new industries to supply its needs. It was to prove the preliminary to the 'occupation' of the hinterlands, to 'fifty years growth in five', and to the recognition of Brazil as 'an emergent world power'.

In this sense the revolution of 1964 was complementary to the transfer of the federal capital to its new location at the Republic's hydrographic centre, where it was liberated from the strong regional influences which had determined and often distorted the course of events in the past. Brasilia became a vantage point on the central plateau of Goias from which to over-view national interests more objectively, in the light of the needs of a vast, disparate and regionally-divided country.

Simmering discontent in the political and financial atmosphere was evident to Leslie Fry soon after his arrival. Brazil had not recovered from the traumatic shock of the unexpected and impulsive abdication of President Janion Quadros in 1960, after only 10 months in office, to create a grave constitutional crisis.

His successor in line was Vice-President Joao Goulart, who had been picked by Quadros to be his running-mate at the presidential elections, despite the fact that he was from the minority opposition P.T.B. (Brazilian Labour Party), whose electoral weight was in the urban trade unions. The traditional parties, Quadros's own U.D.N. (National Democratic Union) and the powerful P.S.D. (Social Democratic Party), which dominated the Federal Congress, represented land-owning interests, industrialists and the Catholic Church. Together with most of the State governors, the two major parties distrusted Goulart because of his record as a radical, and his affiliations with left-wing groups and workers' organisations which were being steadily infiltrated by the Communists. The majority of the armed forces were also opposed to the accession of the vice-president and for much the same reasons.

The impasse between supporters of constitutional legality pledged to the accession of Vice-President Goulart, and the powerful forces opposed to it, was eventually, after days of critical uncertainty, resolved by a constitutional amendment which allowed him to assume the presidency under a parliamentary system patterned on the Westminster model, according to which the incoming administration would be answerable to Congress and not to the Chief Executive.

Once in office President Goulart set out to recover full presidential powers. By appeals to the legalistic traditions of the Brazilian electorate he finally succeeded. By means of a national referendum he freed himself from the straitjacket of congressional control, but at the cost of de-stabilising the political atmosphere once again.

This victory fired his ambitions to succeed himself, and those of his minority P.T.B. party and the radical left to capture power at the next elections.

The wide schism provoked by presidential manoeuvring in pursuit of these objectives was in full swing at the time of the new ambassador's arrival on the scene.

Attempts to mobilise the peasantry of the north-eastern States into politically-motivated organisations, illegal takeover of farmlands, efforts to unionise the non-commissioned officers in the armed forces to bring them under the control of the C.G.T. (National Confederation of Trade Unions), official encouragement to radical student movements, and the premature retirement of senior army commanders to make way for generals picked for their political affiliations and personal loyalty to President Goulart, alarmed the middle-class groups who had opposed the succession of a P.T.B. vice-president in the first place.

Against this background, a rate of inflation approaching 100 per cent. per annum, and the news that Carlos Prestes, the veteran leader of the Brazilian Communist Party (P.C.B.), had returned from a visit to Moscow with a mandate to put his followers behind Goulart and his ambitions, it was no surprise that industrialists, landowners, the Church and the two majority parties joined forces against what was fast becoming a populist bid for power, in which the constitutionalist processes which had allowed Goulart to succeed Quadros would almost inevitably be flouted.

While themselves mounting an anti-Communist crusade in the press and from the pulpit, and setting up clandestine anti-Communist action groups, the Right focused its hope on the military. But the Army, while making contingency plans for meeting an emergency, refused to intervene in a political situation and against the legal regime without convincing evidence that this was what the majority of the nation wanted.

The situation continued to deteriorate during the early part of 1964, until by mid-March President Goulart was losing control and drifting fast into the hands of his extremists.

Matters came to a head on 15th March when, at a mass rally in Rio, and surrounded by leading Communists and trade union leaders, President Goulart called for extra-constitutional solutions including the occupation of farmlands by the workers. Shortly afterwards he committed himself even more deeply by failure to discipline the leaders of naval mutineers barricading themselves in the headquarters of the Communist-led Union of Engineering Workers in Rio de Janeiro. To make matters worse, he was present at another rally a few days later to welcome the released mutineers, to whom he granted an amnesty, at which he delivered further challenges to the established constitutional order.

Even then the Army, having shifted their position from a defensive to a positive stance, remained hesitant. The generals were finally persuaded to move after mass street demonstrations by hundreds of thousands of civilians in three of the country's biggest cities. Bearing banners worded 'for God, Country and Family', they paraded peacefully from the main squares to the cathedrals in protest against the dangerous drift to unconstitutional radicalism by the President.

With the country already verging on anarchy and chaos, and with ample evidence of wide public support, General Castelo Branco, Chief of Army Staff and appointed leader of the military movement, gave the word of command. The garrison of the State of Minas Gerais began their march on Rio on 31st March. They were soon joined by the Rio-based First Army. The following day the Second Army of Sao Paulo declared its support together with the Third Army of the North-East, as, after some hesitation, did the Fourth Army of Rio Grande do Sul, Goulart's home State.

In 48 hours it was all over, without a shot being fired or a life lost. President Goulart fled to Uruguay followed by some of his closest advisers. Congress, with evident relief, confirmed General Castelo Branco as the Revolution's first President, before being itself suspended under a law passed by itself giving him far-reaching emergency powers to do so.

Quite a lot of rough justice was meted out by the Military to those they held responsible for forcing them to take the action they had reluctantly and at the last moment been compelled to take in deference to wide public demand.

But the punitive phase was soon over as the new government devoted itself to what it called 'house cleaning', bringing a runaway inflation under control, and restoring political and economic order. This was quickly achieved, and before the end of the year President Castelo Branco felt able to rescind the more draconian decrees. Press censorship was abolished, Congress re-opened, and work started on drafting a new constitution, proof against the dangers from which the country had almost miraculously escaped.

After two years in office President Castelo Branco stepped down to make way for his successor. He was another general, Marshal Artur da Costa e Silva, the Minister of War and the Army's choice. Inheriting from his predecessor a new Constitution designed to restore civil rule, the situation ran away with him in 1968 when the extreme Left made another bid for power.

Street rioting caused the return of the military to the barracks to be deferred, this time indefinitely. President Costa e Silva, who died of a stroke in 1969, was succeeded by General Emilio Garrastaza Medici. And when he stepped down in turn at the end of his term General Geisel became the fourth president of the 1964 Revolution, to illustrate that it is often more difficult to restore government to the politicians than to take it away from them.

By this time Leslie Fry had left Brazil. But his verdict on the dramatic events of 1964, and the 18 months which elapsed between the revolution of 31st March and his own departure, remained unchanged in retirement as recorded in his personal tribute to President Castelo Branco after his tragic death in a plane crash in 1967.

In common with his diplomatic colleagues, Leslie Fry was a witness and not in any way a participant in the upheaval. Despite retrospective claims to the contrary, even the Americans were passive spectators to a development which changed Brazil's course and put it on the path of destiny.

In fact, in their anxiety to be associated with what was quickly seen as a successful move to counter subversion and a dangerous shift to the Left in the most important republic of Latin America, Washington disregarded the appeal from revolutionaries to stand aside. And they embarrassed the new regime by the haste with which they granted it diplomatic recognition, thereby furnishing useful ammunition to international Communism, which promptly took advantage of the impulsiveness of the U.S. State Department to label the Castelo Branco regime an American stooge brought to power through the machinations of the C.I.A. and the Pentagon.

In common with his American colleague, Leslie Fry had little reliable advance information about the coup. He regarded his role as an observer of what he regarded, rightly as it proved in the end, a strictly Brazilian affair with no outside intervention, and it was in this sense that he reported the course of events in his despatches to London.

The cool detachment of the British Embassy, which contrasted with the urge of the Americans to climb on the Right-wing revolutionary bandwagon, did no disservice to British diplomacy. Some of Castelo Branco's closest advisers, involved as they were in dangerous events forced upon them by circumstances, were anxious to have the benefit of some of what they called the 'ancient wisdom of the English' about the rightness of their course.

Sir Leslie Fry naturally could neither be consulted officially nor speak on behalf of Her Majesty's Government. But through discreet channels and without committing his government he was able to convey some reassurances to the new regime.

It was a kind of commonsense diplomacy in which the ambassador used his own discretion, using trusted third channels for reassuring sincere men engaged, against their will, in what they regarded as the patriotic task of saving their country from financial disaster, anarchy and Marxist Communism. The tide of revolution did, however, wash up on the

Embassy steps one or two delicate problems which Leslie Fry handled with his customary diplomatic tact. One of these arose from the death of President Kennedy.

On the evening of the assassination, 22nd November 1963, the Frys were holding a big reception at the residence, for which invitations had gone out weeks before. To cancel the reception on the strength of rumour would have been a mistake. It was not until about 5.30 p.m. Rio time that Sir Leslie received reliable information that the American President was dead. A member of his staff was driving past the U.S. Embassy as the flag was lowered to half-mast confirming clear confirmation.

Holding the reception in the circumstances was unthinkable. Notifying hundreds of guests in the time available that it was cancelled was an impossibility. Turning away guests at the door would be an embarrassment to say nothing of the congestion in the streets nearby, where jams prevailed even in normal circumstances, and there would have been a traffic nightmare of majestic proportions.

As luck would have it, the broadcasting services were on strike, and not only would most of the guests be unaware of the death of President Kennedy, but the use of the broadcasting stations to inform them of the cancellation of the British Embassy reception was ruled out.

There was, however, one station on the air. This was the government-owned Education and Cultural Service. A telephone call to the Director, Sra Maria Yedda de Leite Linhares, brought instant co-operation. From six o'clock to seven o'clock Radio de Educacáo e Cultura announced every five minutes that the British Embassy reception had been cancelled, and the reason. Only a handful of guests turned up, and an awkward situation was avoided.

When the 31st March rebellion broke out four months later, Maria Yedda was hounded from her post and forced into hiding by a personal and political enemy taking advantage of the disturbed situation. It also happened that in the meantime she had accepted an invitation to visit Britain as the guest of the Foreign Office, as member of a party of distinguished Brazilian ladies holding responsible positions in public life.

While the ambassador, in accordance with British diplomatic practice, was unable to offer her the political asylum she requested, he was able to help her in another way.

Having been suspended from her post, her political rights abrogated under the security laws, and threatened with arrest, it was taken for granted that she would be unable to travel to England because an exit permit would be withheld, or that the British invitation would be withdrawn because of the changed political situation.

Leslie Fry would have none of this. Holding that Her Majesty's Government does not go back on an invitation, he arranged for discreet and unofficial intervention on her behalf at high level with the new military government. Leave of absence, always necessary for everybody in government service—Sra Leite Linhares was still holding her post as Professor of Modern History at the National University—and permission to travel abroad were granted.

She arrived in London a few days after her fellow guests to make the first-ever official three-week visit of a party composed exclusively of ladies from another country a great success.

Another example of skilful *behind*-the-scenes diplomacy by Leslie Fry, it paid useful dividends. It was no disservice to Anglo-Brazilian relations. Britain's insistence on honouring an invitation extended when circumstances were different was recognised by those in the know, both on the ousted Left and in the new regime, that the British Embassy honoured a pledge.

As the dust of revolution settled and tranquillity was restored under President Castelo Branco's firm rule, diplomatic activities returned to normal as the new administration set about clearing up the mess. The Frys renewed the social and ceremonial routine, and started planning their programme of travel to get to know the country to begin after leave at home in the U.K. in late 1965 and early 1966. Their aims were to be disappointed. Notified of his coming retirement, there was little to be done other than keeping the rather dampened-down Anglo-Brazilian fires burning in anticipation of a renewal of the march forward in Brazil and solutions to Britain's economic difficulties.

But it was far from a wholly stagnant period. The ritual ambassadorial attendance at British Chamber of Commerce meetings, the annual banquets of the St. George and St. Andrew's societies, the dinners of the local branch of the British Legion—which Sir Leslie addressed no less than four times in his time in Brazil—continued. Speeches of thanks on being made an honorary member of the Rio de Janeiro Fire Brigade—originally a British creation—and of the Brazilian Academy of Fine Arts, prize days at British schools, presentation of gifts to Brazilian universities and other similar occasions are of interest only for the way they illustrate the life of an ambassador in a country where Britain is held in high esteem on past and present record.

On these occasions, Leslie Fry, who was far from claiming any special gifts as an orator, delivered felicitous, but usually brief speeches. Evidence that he took pains in preparing them is shown by the drafts of some of them preserved among his personal papers.

Uneventful diplomatically, the moving at a snail's pace in trade and commerce as Britain struggled with recurrent financial crises which discouraged export credits for, or investment in, Brazil, Leslie Fry's time, when not spent in performing the regulation duties of all British ambassadors—so much of whose time is a waiting game except in times of crisis—had also to be turned to dealing with a series of unhappy events effecting his own staff. The Commercial Minister, John Wardle Smith, whose health had been poor since arrival in a post to which in the opinion of many he should never have been sent, became very ill and had to be flown home virtually on a stretcher. Margaret Clibborn, wife of the Political Counsellor, Donovan Clibborn, died tragically after undergoing minor surgery. Another member of Chancery staff had to be repatriated because of a breakdown.

While hard pressed by these untoward events Leslie Fry himself had to undergo a major operation. But denuded of some of his key staff he returned quickly to his office, in defiance of the advice of his doctor, with a hospital nurse in constant attendance for several weeks.

But these were accepted as challenges. What caused some distress to Sir Leslie, as the time of departure approached, was the conviction that he was leaving what he later described as 'the most congenial post we have had', in a country which has 'seemed a bed of roses to my wife and me after four troubled years in Indonesia and before that three years in Hungary at an unusually difficult time in that country's history', with a task uncompleted.

Later in retirement he became more philosophical, as he witnessed a recurrence of political trouble in Brazil under Marshal Castelo Branco's successor. It was in 1968-69 under President Costa e Silva that the country experienced what was to prove the world's first outbreak of political terrorism. The draconian measures employed by the military regime to suppress this ugly phenomenon had two unhappy consequences. It arrested the gradual move back to civil rule, and largely through the propagandist campaign mounted by the many political prisoners released into exile to ransom kidnapped ambassadors in Rio, the reputation of Brazil suffered badly in many countries of Europe.

But Leslie Fry's fondness for, and faith in, Brazil and its people remained undimmed in his retirement, as witnessed by his collection of notes and press cuttings about the country in which he last served. The sudden collapse of the terrorist movement after less than three years, after much more cost of life and property than the unending violence in Northern Ireland, offered evidence, as he was wont to explain to friends and visitors, that the enduring underlying forces at work in Brazil in the 1960s and 1970s were those that produced the 'economic miracle' of five successive years of 10 per cent. growth in the economy, and not those of revolution.

Far from blind to the deficiences in the disparities of wealth and the absence of working processes of a modern democracy, yet recognising an uniquely successful exercise in racial harmony, he was the pragmatic 'inglés' in his interpretation of the Brazilian scene as he saw it in his three years in the country.

It was this characteristic, which Brazilians associate with many Englishmen who have lived and worked in their country in the last

100 years and more, that attracted many of them—visiting statesmen, retired ambassadors, and students studying in London—down to Sussex, where Leslie and Penelope Fry kept an ever-open door to their friends. The fact that they were not long enough in Brazil to master the language detracted nothing from the warmth of their hospitality, and never stood in the way of an instinctive empathy between them and the people of a country to which both had clearly become deeply attached.

With its eight and a quarter million square kilometres of territory, a population rising to the 100 million mark in the mid-'sixties, and comprising five very· large and distinct geographic regions, Brazil is more a continent than a country. A lifetime is not enough to know all about it. True understanding can only come through instinct and a readiness to learn without prejudice. These were the qualities Leslie Fry brought to the task, and which made him a partisan of Brazil to a degree for which he was prone to offer excuses as going occasionally beyond the objectivity required of a professional British Ambassador.

*　　*　　*　　*　　*

Addenda sent to *The Times* on the death of Marshal Castelo Branco

Marshal Humberto de Alencar Castelo Branco, former President of Brazil, was a remarkable man, too little known outside his own country for the great contribution he made to its stability and thus to the stability of Latin America.

Brazil under Senhor Goulart's Administration had reached the edge of political chaos and financial ruin by the end of March 1964. So the Army, by tradition the ultimate custodians of national values and basic liberties, intervened. Supported by the Governors of the most important States of Brazil, the leaders of the Armed Services carried through a bloodless revolution in something under three days.

The new President, Marshal Castelo Branco, had been Chief of Army Staff before the revolution. Hardly less important, he had been an outstandingly successful Commandant of the *Escola Superior Da Guerra*, where men prominent in other professions study their country's problems together with senior officers of the Armed Services: it is said that without notice he could deliver any lecture in the curriculum as ably as the regular lecturer. He was a donnish soldier, a teacher as well as a leader, whose opinions on matters of national importance were respected far beyond military circles.

President Castelo Branco's Administration, composed of non-political Party technocrats, offered Brazil a stability and financial integrity not provided by the system which it supplanted. It set an example of honesty in public life, introduced or legislated for a considerable number of long-overdue reforms, including the replacement of the country's outmoded political Party system with two or three Parties of national stature, and did much to allay, though it failed to cure, Brazil's financial ills. But because of the military source of its power, its austere financial and other reformist policies and its measures to ensure that the revolutionary regime should continue, it inevitably brought upon itself unpopularity.

To outward appearances this did not disturb President Castelo Branco. His duty as he saw it was to carry out a corrective task, and in the nature of things he therefore must expect to be unpopular. Without tarnishing that admirable sentiment, however, much more attention might well have been paid to public relations; but this was not in Castelo Branco's ascetic character, unusually reserved by Brazilian standards and devoid of flamboyance.

Of President Castelo Branco's sincere belief in the merits of democracy there need be no question. It was he who insisted, contrary to strong advice from many of his colleagues, that elections for the Governorships of 11 States should go forward in 1965, though the results were bound to reflect the unpopularity of the Federal Government; and it was on his insistence that he was excluded by law from appearing as the regime's candidate in the Presidential elections of 1966.

Brazil's problem over democracy, as he explained in a public speech, was to him obvious enough: given a relatively unsophisticated electorate and—in his view—no responsible political Party system, how were fully democratic processes to be followed if at the same time the country's stability and progress were to be maintained? The problem is not unique to Brazil.

Marshal Castelo Branco had a high regard for the British Commander-in-Chief and soldiers with whom he had served as a senior Staff Officer of the Brazilian Division in Italy during the Second World War, and above all he was a great admirer of Sir Winston Churchill, whom he had met in the course of an inspection by the Prime Minister of Allied Forces. On Sir Winston's death, President Castelo Branco at once made known his wish to attend the Memorial Service at the Anglican Church in Rio de Janeiro, to which in the event he was accompanied by his entire Cabinet. Later in 1965, on Commonwealth Day, he and his Ministers dined at Her Majesty's Embassy and afterwards saw some films concerned with Sir Winston's life and funeral. From his comments it appeared that, of all the triumphs and vicissitudes of the Prime Minister's career, none had impressed him more deeply than the manner in which Sir Winston had accepted defeat in the first post-war elections. 'That', said Castelo Branco, 'was a lesson in democracy to us all.'

Leslie Fry
23 July 1967

INDEX

By R. Chamard